# GUILDFORD
## THE CHANGING FACE

STANLEY NEWMAN

breedon **books**
PUBLISHING

First published in Great Britain in 2002 by
The Breedon Books Publishing Company
Limited
Breedon House, 3 The Parker Centre,
Derby, DE21 4SZ.

ISBN 1 85983 313 6

Printed and bound by Butler & Tanner, Frome,
Somerset, England.

Cover printing by Lawrence-Allen Colour
Printers, Weston-super-Mare, Somerset.

# Contents

In Memory

of

Fred and Mary

# Introduction

FROM the quiet Surrey market town where I was born and spent my youth Guildford has become, in more recent years, a major commercial centre with a vibrant hub of entertainment.

I have always been proud to call Guildford my home town and feel it is a wonderful place to live and work. Most of the changes I have witnessed, in and around the town over the past 50 years or so, have been for the better, although during the 1960s and 1970s there came a period when I think the planners seemed to 'lose the plot'. The same, however, could probably be said about most towns at that time. This is when I really became more aware and interested in the town where I lived, particularly as some of the fine old buildings were being destroyed. During this period many people were dismayed by the unattractive buildings being erected in place of what had stood before.

In 1970, with my trusty old camera, I began to photograph buildings about to be demolished or in the process of being removed. My information and collection of pictures started then and I am thankful that other people, of like mind, also cared enough about 'our town' to keep records and photographs. There are times today when I think we need to stop rushing around, to reflect and remember Guildford as it was, not over a period of 100 years but just a few decades past, to events and places with which many people can relate.

The majority of photographs in this book cover the past 50 years, with a few taken in the 21st century. Older pictures are also included, where appropriate, to cover a certain topic. *Guildford: The Changing Face*, although not a history book, does include a few historical facts relating to the town's ancient buildings. It shows the visual changes made to many of our buildings and locations and there are pages which give past and present views.

Not only have the façades of the buildings changed, but also their use, for example the 1913 Electricity Works now The Electric Theatre.

There are sections covering many of our public houses which have been lost or had their names changed over the years. Photographs are also included which depict modern Guildford, the leisure activities and some of the societies within the town. The charm of Guildford is not only its location, buildings, river and surrounding countryside but also the people we meet and with whom we share our lives. A few of these people are mentioned at the end of this book.

The ambition to compile this book would not have been realised without the help of a number of people. My grateful thanks go to two very special people, who have been such a great help in the compilation of the book. My wife June for her assistance in reading and typing the text and her understanding and encouragement throughout. Also to my good friend Tom Wilkie, whose 1960s photographs are surely some of the best ever taken of Guildford. Tom is now living a quiet life and no longer has anything to do with photography, having sold his business complete with equipment and records. In addition, David Rose, from whom I gained the incentive to start the book, after reading *Images of Guildford* which he jointly compiled with Graham Collyer, and his own *Memory Lane Guildford and District*, deserves my special thanks for his inspiration and advice.

Whilst compiling this book I have met people for the first time who have freely given their time to help with information or generously allowed me to use their photographs.

I would like to thank John Sutton for passing on his knowledge of Guildford and for the loan of his photographs.

My thanks go to other people who have helped with information including Alan Slater of Guildford Model Engineering Society, Kirsty Kilpatrick from Disability Challengers, Manisha Thaker at Electric Theatre, Paul Tester of Lampard & Partners Co Ltd, and Claude Wilkins.

I should also like to thank the following people for allowing me to use their photographs: Margaret Moore, Steven Lampard, Miss Mumford, Brian and Sylvia Wheeler, William and Ruth Bakewell, Reg Gould, David Bennett, Mark Sturley, Jean Lampard, Norman Hamshere, Nikolai Demenko, Pieter Betlem, Bill Broberg, Bill and Doreen Bellerby, Baroness Sharp, James Wakefield of Spectrum Leisure Centre, Steve Porter of the *Surrey Advertiser* and Peter Ferris.

Finally my thanks go to Justin White of Repropoint Reprographic Services, Park Road, Guildford, for his patience and excellent service; also to manager Clive Plant for his understanding. I do hope you enjoy this look at Guildford and gain pleasure not only from pictures of the past but also those of more recent times.

Stanley Newman
Guildford
Summer 2002

# Around and About

## The Guildhall

The Guildhall frontage has not changed in over 300 years. With its clock projecting over the High Street, it is the building most regarded as the main symbol of the town.

The Guildhall clock was made by John Alward, a London clockmaker. It is generally accepted that he presented it to the Guild Merchants in 1683 in exchange for permission to set up a shop in the borough. The mechanism for the clock is actually installed in the Guildhall roof and has to be wound-up three times a week.

The present bell for the clock dates from 1931. The original bell, which is said to have come from St Martha's Church, can now be seen in entrance lobby to the Guildhall.

For centuries the Guildhall held many different court sessions in its Main Hall. These included Assizes, County Quarter Sessions, County Court and modern Crown Court. The judge looked out on to a courtroom with splendid pine panelling. A sign on the wall faced the jury and advised them to 'Be Just and Fear Not'.

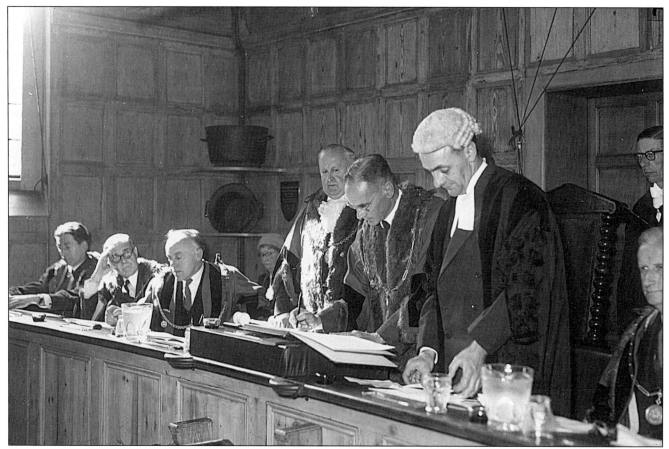

In 1957 the Guildhall was used for the ceremony to grant the Freedom of the Borough of Guildford to Alderman L. Powell, with Mayor Harold Kimber looking on.

The Council Chamber, on the first floor, has a door leading to the balcony which overlooks the High Street. Guildford's civic plate can be seen in secure cabinets in the hall.

A view from the Guildhall balcony of a craft market during the July 2001 Guildford Summer Festival.

The Guildhall underwent extensive restoration work in 1986-7. This was carried out by Lampard & Partners, a local building contractor from Albury. One of the jobs was to strip down, clean and colour match the pine panels. Well-seasoned pitch pine, obtained from the closed Dennis Brothers Woodbridge Hill Works, was used to replace panels where necessary. The entrance hall, shown above, had new wood installed to match the main hall.

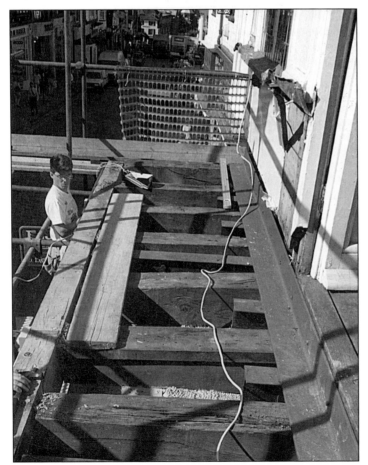

There were extensive repairs to the balcony, which included new lead work.

The stairs originally lead to a passageway which joined the courtroom with the cells in North Street's old police station. This picture also shows pipes which were for the installation of a new central heating system.

# Abbot's Hospital

My favourite Guildford building is the Hospital of the Blessed Trinity, better known as Abbot's Hospital, built essentially in a Tudor design with a beautiful gatehouse tower and courtyard. The High Street frontage is especially pleasing to the eye, balanced on either side by the wings with their Dutch-style gables. Abbot's Hospital was founded by George Abbot in 1619. He was Archbishop of Canterbury and a distinguished son of Guildford.

In fact, it is not a hospital at all but an almshouse for old Guildfordians. Originally it provided residential accommodation for 12 men and eight widows or spinsters who had to be 'Guildford folk of good character' and over the age of 60.

Above the entrance, on second floor, is the Monmouth Room where the Duke of Monmouth was kept prisoner for one night in 1685 on the way to his execution in London after his defeat at the Battle of Sedgemoor.

George Abbot was born in 1562, in a small cottage near the Town Bridge. A car-park occupies this site today. Abbot attended Guildford Grammar School and then went on to Oxford University. By the time George Abbot graduated from Balliol College in 1585, he had received his Master of Arts degree. He was appointed to several posts at the University, from Junior Dean in 1587 to Vice-Chancellor in 1600, 1603 and 1605. He was ordained into the Church and in 1609 became Bishop of Coventry and Lichfield. In 1611 he achieved the position of Primate of all England, the Archbishop of Canterbury.

Some of the residents pictured in the courtyard at Abbot's Hospital in 1975.

The boardroom, Abbot's Hospital.

The banqueting room on the first floor, known as Guesten Hall, has an original oak dining table and stools. The picture of the lady and two children is believed to be by Guildford artist John Russell.

Over the fireplace in Guesten Hall is an interesting carved oak mantelpiece. It illustrates the hall's purpose, with four figures representing a carver, a servitor, a cup bearer and an usher. Between them are carvings of a jester and two entertainers.

A portrait of Archbishop Abbot, by a student of Paul Van Somer, hangs in the boardroom which is above entrance to Abbot's Hospital.

George Abbot died in 1633, at his rural palace in Croydon, and his body was brought back to Guildford for burial. His tomb is in Holy Trinity Church, opposite Abbot's Hospital.

The garden of Abbot's Hospital, pictured from North Street before work started on an extension to add more accommodation. There was a local objection to the scheme to build 12 flats in the garden. However, after a public enquiry, the Department of the Environment approved the plans in 1980.

The new wing, built in 1983 in the 17th-century garden backing on to North Street, allowed the hospital's governors to provide modern accommodation for residents. There is now accommodation for 24 people including two flats for married couples.

The small chapel, where residents were required to attend daily prayers, now has morning services on Mondays, Wednesdays and Fridays. The two stained-glass windows are large in proportion to the chapel and were probably brought in from another building.

# The High Street Undercroft

Lampard and Partners, who specialise in working on old and listed properties in Guildford, have often faced quite a challenge. In 1989 they undertook restoration of the 13th-century undercroft beneath the Halifax Building Society at 72 High Street. The picture above shows one of the medieval pillars before restoration. Also pictured are the 50-year-old brick piers which were removed and replaced with skilfully designed steel structures.

Iron bands were fitted by the Victorians to strengthen the pillar and during the restoration it was decided to keep them as they were part of the Undercroft's history. To save cutting into the walls, all lighting was fitted into the floor. English Heritage considered the undercroft to be 'the finest medieval building of its kind'.

# The Royal Grammar School

The building of the Royal Grammar School started in 1557 and continued throughout the 16th century. The famous chained library contains 85 volumes, many of which are rare early books. Another claim to fame is that the earliest mention of the game of cricket occurs in connection with the Grammar School. In one of the corporation court books there is a passage which describes 'Creckett' being played, in about 1558 by scholars of the Free School, as the Grammar School was sometimes called.

The passage read:

Encroachment on the waste ground; enquiry at The Court leet January 1598. Court Book 1586-1675.

Open at the end of the evidence of John Derrick, one of the Coroners for Surrey, aged 59, he deposed that he knew the land in question (at the top of North Street) for the last 50 years and that it was used by the inhabitants to lay timber for Sawpitsand that Ould Butler, a Carpenter deceased, did commonly use to make fames of timber there and also this deponent saith that, being a Scholar in the Free Schoole of Guildford, hee and diverse of his fellowes did runne and play there at creckett and other plaies.

This famous passage contains the first occurrence of the word 'cricket' in the English Language and is evidence for the existence of the game some 50 years before the date of the enquiry itself.

The Chained Library which contains one book published in 1440 and several others printed in the 15th century. A Guildford man, John Parkhurst, who became Bishop of Norwich in 1560, bequeathed most of the books to the library.

The Great Chamber in 2001, with the names of famous old boys carved on the beams. The Old School is now mainly used for music lessons.

On 2 December 1962, a fire gutted the East Wing of the old Grammar School building, the former Usher's House. The staircase and roof collapsed and many books in the library were ruined either by smoke or water. Fortunately books in the Chained Library escaped with only slight smoke damage. It was not until 1965 that restoration work was completed and the Duchess of Gloucester formally reopened the building on 9 June that year.

The rear of the Grammar School building during the fire of 1962 and, below, as it was in the 1880s.

## Guildford House

No 25 High Street, which later became no 155, has had a diverse life. It was built by lawyer John Child in 1660. From 1736 until 1839 it was home to the Martyr family. In 1844, 25 High Street was a commercial premises with Frank Apted, cooper and sacking manufacturer, in residence. Various tradesmen occupied the house up until 1928, when the Lambert Tea Room and Grill opened. This did not survive long as Nuthall's acquired the building in 1929 and opened their restaurant in 1930. Nuthall's was a popular restaurant and venue for wedding receptions up until its closure in 1957, when Guildford Corporation purchased the property. It is now one of the town's treasures. As Guildford House Gallery it shows numerous art collections. It also holds many exhibitions from ceramics to wedding dresses and all admission is free.

On top of all the square oak newel posts stand urns carved with fruits and flowers.

The Georgian staircase of Nuthall's Restaurant in 1957.

# Nuthalls
## 17th Century Building
## 25 HIGH STREET, GUILDFORD
LICENSED RESTAURANT, LUNCHEONS, TEAS
CONFECTIONERY MADE ON THE PREMISES
RECEPTIONS, PARTIES, *Enquiries Invited*

A 1950s advertisement for Nuthall's.

The closure of Nuthall's Restaurant in 1957 brought to an end 27 years of service to the town.

On the first floor, the Powell Room at the front of the house has a very ornate plaster ceiling dating back to the 17th century. It is regarded as one of the finest in the south of England. This photograph of the ceiling was taken in 1957, at the time it was Nuthall's Restaurant. The ceiling was restored in 1992 when general restoration work was carried out on the house.

Remarkably, many of the elaborate wrought-iron window catches are original 17th-century fasteners.

These photographs (above and below), taken during the restoration of Guildford House in 1992, show part of the superb staircase carved in elm and oak. For many years it had been covered with layers of paint but this was removed and the exposed wood sealed and polished.

This picture of the first-floor landing shows the beautifully carved balustrade panels which rise from the ground floor and continue up to the second floor. Also shown is the elegant arcading around the landing and decorative balusters.

## The changing backs of Guildford House.

*Above left:* In 1957, when the building was occupied by Nuthall's Restaurant, with concrete steps to the garden.

*Above:* Taken after renovations in 1992, this photograph shows that the doorway has been bricked up and made good with hanging tiles that look like bricks to match existing 17th-century tiles.

*Left:* In 2001 the building is again serving refreshments, even though this takes place only on the lower ground floor and outside on the patio, weather permitting.

# Tunsgate

A rare picture taken of Tunsgate Arch before the pillars were moved apart in 1935, to make easier access between High Street and Tunsgate.

This photograph was taken in 1985 when you could still drive into the High Street from Tunsgate.

What a difference 50 years has made to Tunsgate. This 1948 photograph shows the Baptist Chapel at the end of the road next to the cottages with their washing hanging on the line. The original road was not much wider than the path. The cleared area was made into a car-park.

Tunsgate on a quiet Sunday in 2001.

The Baptist Chapel, which restricted the top end of Tunsgate to a single carriageway, was demolished in 1954 and in 1974 Commercial Road Baptist Church was closed. A new church opened in Millmead and it became known as the Millmead Centre Baptist Church.

Tunsgate in 1975 with, on the left, Jeffery's Motor Cycles in the building once occupied by the Three Tuns beer house which closed in the 1930s. At one time the landlord was a Mr W. Boozer.

# Sydenham Road

Sydenham Road has changed considerably in the last 50 years. Previously it was known as South Road. In the 1950s Charlotteville Youth Club was held at Pewley School, now the Adult Education Centre. After club, members would call in to Steven's fish and chip shop which is now the site of the Castle car-park. Sometimes they would first visit the Robin Hood public house on the way. Gilbert, the landlord, had to climb a few steps to collect drinks from a back room. This often resulted in shandies being spilled on his way back to the bar. No one asked for 'a top-up' because Gilbert, who was a great chap, would have struggled back up the steps. By the time he returned it would have been too late for fish and chips.

These cars are parked outside the Robin Hood, which was situated at the junction of Sydenham Road and Bright Hill when this photograph was taken in 1960. The alterations to Bright Hill moved the junction away from the pub. It also removed 23 houses in Bright Hill, 28 in Hill Place and these houses in Sydenham Road.

A view from the top of Bright Hill in 1958, showing gas holders prominent in the town. In contrast, we see the unfinished cathedral on Stag Hill surrounded by trees and fields. The Robin Hood public house can be seen at the bottom of the hill on the left.

The Robin Hood now stands alone surrounded by parked cars in 2001. The Pewley School building, previously the Central School, is on the left.

The Queen's Head public house, South Street, in the early 1900s.

The Queen's Head building in 1959, then occupied by Stent & Co, printers. The street had by then become known as Sydenham Road.

These buildings were demolished in 1959 to make way for the Sydenham Road multi-storey car-park.

This photograph, taken from the top of Guildford Castle Keep, shows Sydenham Road car-park under construction in 1962. Tunsgate Square was built on the open car-park; Candy Corner had already been demolished for road widening.

The finished building was never very popular. Some people thought the design too austere.

Sydenham Road car-park opened in 1963, but you could still park outside the Royal Oak. F.H. Billimore & Son's builder's yard stretched from Oxford Road to Oxford Terrace.

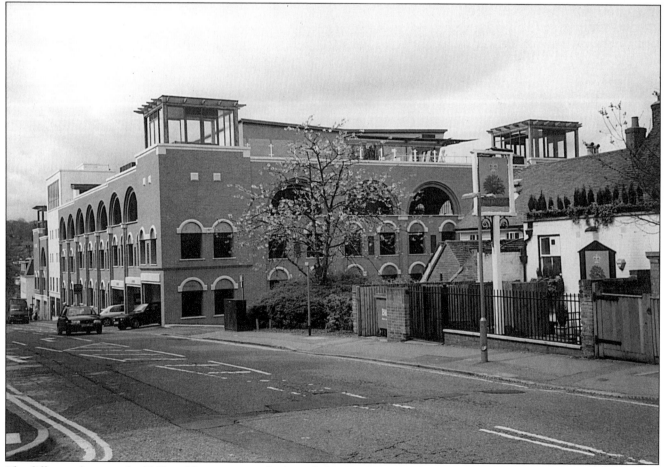

The difference between the 1963 multi-storey car-park pictured above and new Castle car-park, pictured here in 2001, illustrates the improvements in the aspect of buildings erected today, from the unsightly architecture of the 1960s.

# The Castle Grounds

There is not much left of Guildford Castle except the keep and odd sections of wall. What we do have, though, is the beautiful Castle Grounds, a peaceful haven just a few steps from the busy High Street. It is generally believed that Guildford Castle was built in the 12th century, in the reign of Henry II. He spent Christmas here in 1186. In 1216, the castle was taken by Prince Louis of France, who had invaded England by invitation of the Barons in Arms against King John. The French withdrew after John's death later in the year. King John and Henry III stayed in Guildford Castle many times, John over 100 times. During Henry III's reign the castle was used as a prison and this continued until about 1612.

Castle Arch, the gateway to Guildford Castle, originally had a portcullis. In the wall today you can still see where it moved up and down. Prince Henry died at the castle in 1274, aged seven, while he was staying with his grandmother, Queen Eleanor of Provence. His parents, Edward I and Eleanor of Castille, had his heart placed in a casket and kept it at the Dominion Friary, now site of Friary Shopping Centre. Today, the Castle Grounds is a place to sit and rest awhile and admire the immaculate gardens, bowling green and old keep.

In this 1960s photograph can be seen the unfinished cathedral between the keep and the trees. On the right of the picture is the chimney of the old indoor swimming baths which was demolished in 1972.

The Sundial Memorial to Edward and Eleanor faces the Castle Grounds where their son, Prince Henry, died in 1274.

Today in the Castle Grounds, seats, such as the ones shown here, can be donated and dedicated in memory of loved ones.

The formal opening of the Castle Grounds in 1888 was performed by the mayor, William Swayne, and Lord Midleton. Guildford's borough surveyor Henry Peak, designed the layout of the grounds around the keep and bowling green.

Today, concerts are performed by visiting bands on most Sunday afternoons throughout the summer. Theatrical companies also present a season of plays on the bandstand.

Castle Grounds entrance in 1963.

The bowling green was shown on a map of Guildford dated 1739. This photograph was taken in 1974 when the draughtboards were in regular use.

Unfortunately the games of draughts were stopped because of damage to the bowling area caused by vandals.

This sculpture of *Alice Through The Looking Glass* is situated in a small garden within the Castle Grounds. It was created by Jeanne Argent, a student at Guildford Adult Education Institute, and presented to Guildford Borough by Municipal General Insurance in 1990. When this picture was taken, in December 2000, children had been enjoying a snowball fight with Alice.

# Quarry Street

Not so many years ago Quarry Street was the main route out of town to Horsham and on the way you passed the oldest part of Guildford, the Saxon tower of St Mary's Church.

Quarry Street backs in early 1950s. The old British Legion building is on the left. The gardens of Quarry Street houses originally reached down to the river bank. With the building of Millbrook car-park and realignment of Millbrook Road, the gardens were lost.

Lower Quarry Street in 1960 with the 19th-century Good Intent beershop, which later became a lodging house, ready for demolition. Martin's garage is on the extreme right.

A 1968 photograph of Rosemary Alley, part of an ancient route which leads down to the river from Quarry Street, across the footbridge to Porridge Pot Alley, then through to the Portsmouth Road.

The Lantern Café, on the corner of Mill Lane and Quarry Street. In 1964 it was run by Miss Margaret Thorne who also had the Bun Shop which was opposite the Odeon Cinema in Epsom Road.

Guildford British Legion Club occupied 14-15 Quarry Street for many years. When they moved to their new premises in Millbrook in 1987, Lampard & Partners converted the buildings into offices.

In 1988 this section of the Quarry Street backs was restored to its former glory. Number 13 is a small 16th-century house built between the larger properties in Quarry Street.

In 1988 workmen, removing plaster from a wall at 13 Quarry Street discovered that it was covering a 16th-century wall painting. It had probably not been seen for centuries. The centrepiece depicts a man in Elizabethan costume carrying a 'waster' which was a thin cudgel. Although the painting was in good condition it did require some restoration work. Today it is protected by a screen to safeguard it for the future.

# North Street

The Yvonne Arnaud Theatre, which opened in June 1965, replaced Guildford Repertory Theatre in North Street, which came to an abrupt end when it was completely destroyed by fire in 1963. The cause of the fire was not known.

Five years earlier there were problems with the ancient central heating system overheating. This caused steam to escape into the auditorium and the heat on stage became overpowering, although actors were happy to continue their rehearsals even though the coke-fired boiler was in the cellar under the stage. Eventually they agreed to the suggestion that it might be a good idea to stop rehearsals until the fire base was removed and the boiler had cooled down. Apparently there was no one person responsible for the boiler, simply a rota system to shovel in coke.

Guildford has had two theatres before the Repertory Theatre opened in the late 1940s. The first theatre, in Market Street, served the town from about 1804 until the mid-19th century. It had a seating capacity for 400 people, although the town had a population of approximately only 3,000 at that time. With the relative size of Guildford today it is interesting that the Yvonne Arnaud Theatre has seating for only about 590 people, but then today there are other distractions.

After the Market Street Theatre closed, Guildford was without a theatre until the Theatre Royal opened in 1912 , in a building occupied by the Co-operative Society and shown in the above photograph.

The Theatre Royal was situated at the junction of North Street and Leapale Road from 1912 until 1932.

The Co-op Corner in 1973.

For the 20 years of its existence, the Theatre Royal offered a variety of entertainment including musicals, revues, farces, dramas and pantomimes. The final production was *Alice in Wonderland* which was attended by the original Alice, Mrs Alice Hargreaves.

The auditorium of the Theatre Royal could seat just over 1,000 people.

Guildford's weekly cattle market was held in the High Street until 1865. It then moved to North Street, a quieter thoroughfare, because of the increase in High Street traffic.

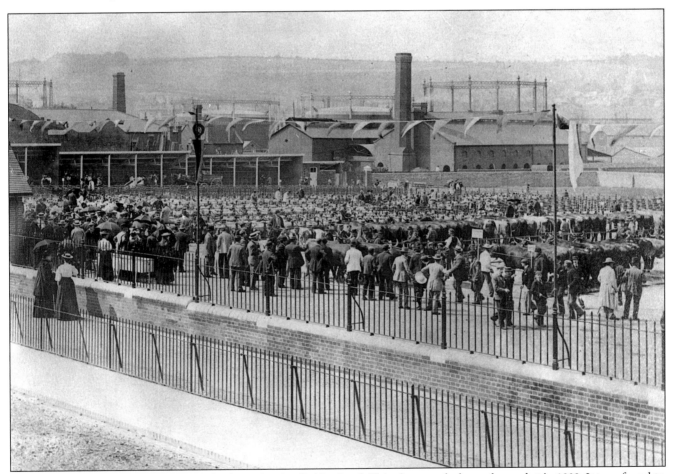

In 1896 the market moved to a purpose-built site in Woodbridge Road. This photograph shows the market in 1902. It transferred to Slyfield in 1969, where it survived until 2000. In 2002 Guildford is without a cattle market.

This was North Street in 1968. Today this market still operates on Fridays and Saturdays, selling fruit and vegetables. Over the years it has expanded and now includes stalls which sell general items.

Pimms furniture store occupied the top of North Street, from North Street Square to the Dolphin public house, and incorporated the 18th-century Northgate House. They were also funeral directors, cabinet makers, upholsterers, carpet layers and decorators and also provided a removal service. The whole site was redeveloped in the 1960s.

An interesting place just off North Street is Quakers Acre, a quiet corner in the town centre nestling between the library and the shops. The Quakers acquired the land in 1672 for their burial ground because church ground was denied them. In 1927, the Society of Friends gave the land to the town as a formal garden.

In Quakers Acre can be seen a plaque dedicated to the memory of the 'Guildford Five', the five young people who lost their lives in the bombing of the Horse and Groom public house on 5 October 1974. They were Carolyn Slater, Peter Craig, Anne Hamilton, William Forsyth and John Hunter.

The Horse and Groom was rebuilt in 1974-5, following the damage from the terrorist bomb. Its reopening in 1975 was a memorable occasion for the town. For commercial reasons it was finally closed in 1992, by which time it had been renamed Grooms. Sadly, North Street has lost six other public houses and two churches in the last 40 years.

In the 1960s the Surrey Arms was a popular pub, especially on market days. Like most public houses at that time, it still had a public bar. It closed in 1985 and is now an outlet of Pizza Hut. Collis Woods was the major music shop of the time, with the Royal Arms Hotel and Restaurant – it was really a café – another favourite meeting place for locals.

The Dolphin was situated on the corner of North Street and Chertsey Street. It was built in *c*.1915 to replace the Dolphin Inn which was a few yards away in Chertsey Street. The building which replaced the Dolphin after its demolition in 1964 is now occupied by TGI Friday.

The Dolphin Inn, which was demolished in 1915-16, was the second public house of that name in Guildford. In the 18th century there was a Dolphin pub in what is now upper High Street, near East Gate Gardens.

In this picture can be seen the entrance to the Berni Inn, next door to Superdrug, which led to a restaurant and bars on the first floor. There was also access from Market Street. It survived in Guildford from 1972 to the early 1990s.

From the early 1800s until 1966, the premises at 36-38 North Street was the home of the Vintner's Arms public house. After the pub closed, the building was retained and converted into shops.

Permission was granted to demolish the Little White Lion in 1983. The building was spared and it also was converted into a shop.

The Blackfriars public house was opened as part of the Friary Centre in 1981 but lasted for only just over seven years until the centre was redeveloped in 1989. The plan was to resite the pub in North Street, but at the time of writing this had not happened.

In 1973, at the lower end of North Street, traffic moved in the opposite direction. The Blackfriars public house was situated approximately in the position of the Mothercare shop on the right.

By the early 1970s, the Congregational Church, the Methodist Church and the old Victorian Post Office building were no longer in North Street.

A 1959 view, from Harvey's roof garden, of the Methodist Church with the tower and chimney of the Friary Brewery to the right.

When this photograph was taken in 1960, it was possible to walk through an archway of the old barracks at the bottom of North Street into Friary Square. You turned right for Onslow Street bus station or walked across the river, via a footbridge, to Farnham Road bus station.

The original barracks were built in the 1850s for the Surrey Militia. It was used for military purposes only until the militia amalgamated with the Queen's Regiment and moved to a new barracks at Stoughton in 1876. Part of the building was converted for residential use. Eventually, business premises occupied the barracks until their demolition in the 1970s.

King Bros, Ayers & Sons Ltd, and Buyers (just visible to the right of the picture), who promised to buy anything, occupied the barrack building in 1960. The sign above the window over Ayers baker's shop reads, 'Durable Plastics Limited, now at new factory, turn left at by-pass.'

Durable Plastics began life in two Nissen huts in Friary Square in 1952, with a staff of four. In 1956 they moved to Woodbridge Meadows and changed their name to Plastic Coating Ltd.

# The Foxenden tunnels

In 1991 Lampard and Partners undertook the work of extending the York Road car-park. This required the removal of 3,700 cubic metres of chalk and the anchoring of the chalk cliff face with stressed steel ties and plates located in existing tunnels which were last used during World War Two as an air-raid shelter.

A rare view of the Foxenden air-raid shelter and first-aid post, pictured during extension work to the car-park. The facilities were quite basic, as can be seen from the picture of the ladies' toilet. The tunnels were bricked up after the war.

In the 1950s it was possible to enter the emergency shafts of the tunnels simply by moving aside a sheet of corrugated iron. The two vertical shafts descend from small brick buildings beside the tennis courts and putting green. Thankfully brickwork now seals these openings. Climbing down the iron ladder for the first time, with just a small torch, was enough to unnerve anybody. You did not know what to expect when you stepped off the last rung. It might be water or just a long drop. Even so it was a great adventure for youngsters. Today the two buildings remain the only visible reminder of the Foxenden tunnels.

# Bridge Street

Tucked between the modern bars in Bridge Street is a boarded-up shop which attracted little attention in 2001. In the 1950 and '60s, though, this was S. & M. Simons, the tailors, a favourite shop of many local lads. His Italian-style suits were our pride and joy with their short jackets and hand-stitched lapels. The Teddy Boys were also very proud of their colourful long jackets and drain-pipe trousers. Contrary to popular belief, there was generally friendly rivalry between the two groups. A Saturday afternoon visit to see Michael Simons – who lived over the shop with his father – to view cloth for a new suit was like meeting a friend for a social occasion. He was always interested in everyone and it could take an hour to answer his enquiries about the lads who were not there at the time. He was a lovely man.

A view of Walnut Tree Close from Bridge Street in 1957, before Bridge House was built.

The same corner six years later, looking towards lower Farnham Road, with Bridge House and the petrol station. Also pictured is the Railway Hotel during its demolition.

## Portsmouth Road

Jackson's cycle shop, shown here in 1959 at the bottom of Portsmouth Road, was the favourite shop for keen cyclists. They kept an amazing stock of spares, new and secondhand cycles and also carried out repairs.

Next to the Cannon Inn was the Guildford Glass and Metal Works, which occupied the old Cannon Brewery buildings. It was demolished in 1960 and the Central Electricity Generating Board offices were built on the site.

This wonderful aerial photograph, taken by Tom Wilkie in 1960, shows how this area of town has changed in the last 40 years. Top left can be seen the railway station with smoke from an engine, waiting maybe to set off for Portsmouth, and the crescent-shaped engine sheds now the site of the Farnham Road car-park. Centre left is the then recently-built CEGB office building at the bottom of Portsmouth Road, which was demolished in 2000. Across the river, Moon's timber yard, soon to be replaced by Plummer's Store, later Debenhams.

Centre of the picture is traffic crossing the Town Bridge, with downstream the footbridge connecting both bus stations. Between the bridges a Wey barge is tied up at the town wharf. Top right is the gas works site where the gas holders have been removed ready for the building of the Bedford Road car-park and the County Courts.

Top centre is Bridge House, which at that time was a year old. Now it has been replaced by a much more acceptable looking building. Centre right can be seen the building of the new Marks and Spencer store in progress in the High Street.

If you look closely you will see many more changes. In the right-hand corner is Quarry Street which has not changed much over the years, with the oldest part of Guildford, the Saxon tower of St Mary's Church, in a prominent position.

# Onslow Street

This photograph of Onslow Street, taken in the late 1890s, shows a Miles & Sutton family outing. Charles Sutton opened an outfitters and drapery shop, under the name Chas Sutton & Co, in about 1893, just a few doors up from the barbers shop seen behind the coach and horses, He later moved to a larger premises across the road at the junction of Onslow Street and Woodbridge Road. Like most shopkeepers at that time, Charles lived with his family over the shop. In the 1950s, Hill's, a furniture shop, took over tenancy of the property until its demolition in 1974.

In 1974 the barber's shop advertisement was still visible on the wall, even though shop had long gone, At that time Heathorns turf accountants occupied the premises. It was one of the last buildings to be demolished in 1977, to make way for the Friary Shopping Centre project.

Onslow Street in 1973 had a one-way traffic system. From the early 1900s Angel Son & Gray Ltd, ironmongers and building material suppliers, had occupied the Onslow Street and Woodbridge Road site. In the 1960s an extension to the store was built, seen on the right. It then became known as Angels of Guildford.

1975 saw the demolition of Angel's Corner along with the Jubilee Social Club. Angel's moved to a new premises in Mary Road.

The ground floor of the Rodboro Buildings is now occupied by Wetherspoons but in 1963 it comprised individual shops. Next to Onslow Street bus station was Stanley Godfrey & Co, who sold used cars, with Jimmy Clayton next door at Clare's supplying all your motor spares. Then there was the larger than life Bert Webb, the turf accountant, Dowdswell's stationers, the Corner Shop selling confectionery, Lamberts the jeweller, and the last shop in the picture is the Guildford Pet Stores. The neglected Rodboro Buildings were at one time definitely under threat of demolition. They were built in 1901 by the Dennis Company especially for car production. It was one of the first purpose-built motor-car works in Britain and the first Dennis fire fighting appliance was made here in 1908. In 1986 it was made a Grade II listed building.

The Old People's Welfare Centre, as it was named in the 1960s, was situated at the back of Onslow Street bus station, next to the electricity works (see *Days of Leisure*). The present Age Concern Riverside Centre overlooks the river close to Friary Bridge.

Safeguard's 1956 AEC Reliance bus, standing in Onslow Street bus station in the late 1950s, with the driver and conductress waiting for their passengers. Safeguard sold this Reliance, registration number 200 APB, in 1962. In 2002, after noticing an advertisement for its sale, Safeguard bought the bus back and brought it home to Guildford.

In Farnham Road bus station, Yellow Bus Services' 1946 Bedford OWB is waiting to leave for Farnham via the pretty route through Puttenham and Cutmill. The bus station snack bar can just be seen behind the vehicle.

Aldershot and District double-decker leaving Farnham Road bus station in 1960.

There is lot to see in this 1965 picture, including the two bus stations with their double-decker buses, and also a bus crossing the Town Bridge. Right of Onslow Street bus station is the Friary Brewery complete with its chimney and tower. Next to it can be seen part of Friary Square with the archway into North Street. On the other side are Rodboro Buildings.

Top right is Harvey's, now House of Fraser, with its roof garden. To the left of Harvey's is the spire of the Methodist Church in North Street, now the site of Barclays Bank. The River Wey can just be seen on the right with no sign yet of the gyratory system or Debenhams store. The long white building is the offices of solicitors Wells & Philpot, now the White House public house. In the foreground is St Nicolas's Church before the new hall was built.

The gas holders, prominent in this 1963 aerial photograph, will be remembered by many as a feature of the town at that time. Most of the gas works buildings had been demolished to make way for the building of the Bedford Road car-park. The site on which the gas holders were situated is now an open car-park. Guildford's 'new' police station and County Courts are now on the site of old Woodbridge Road cattle market, which is shown to the left of the gas holders in this picture. The buildings by the river with the chimney, have now given way to the Crown Courts. Above the cleared area the chimney of the Friary Brewery can be seen with Friary Tower to its left. The brewery was demolished in the early 1970s and in its place we now have the Friary Shopping Centre.

# Park Street

Park Street *c.*1900 with start of one-way system. Note the sign, 'Keep to the left road'. With the width of Park Street in those days there was little else one could do.

Park Street and lower Farnham Road in 1972 with the old Technical College building in the process of being demolished. In the 1950s-60s Surrey County Council used the property as an Education Department and Youth Employment Bureau.

Thirty years on and the view has changed dramatically. Notice how much the road had to be raised to line up with Friary Bridge. Most of the buildings have changed with exception of St Nicolas's Church and Debenhams store, although originally the store was called Plummer's.

# The Town Bridge

In 1985, the 80-year-old Town Bridge was replaced at a cost to Surrey County Council of £250,000. Guildford Borough Council contributed £50,000 to this cost so that the original cast-iron panels and parapets could be retained, and to allow for width of the bridge to stay the same.

## High Street

High Street in 1965, pictured from The Mount, shows an uninterrupted sweep of road down to the river and over the Town Bridge. Today Millbrook Road cuts off High Street from the bridge.

This early 1970s photograph of the High Street shows different degrees of change. Look above the shop fronts and you will see that today there is very little difference. The overall view shows a different picture with two-way traffic, Harvey's of Guildford, which later became Army and Navy Stores and today is House of Fraser, International stores and Timothy White's the chemist which have both closed after being part of the High Street scene for many years.

The premises of John Collier was the only building to survive after the extension to Millbrook Road in 1973. Shops next to the Town Bridge were all demolished. The bridge became free of traffic for the first time since 1754. Then, coaches and carriages were allowed access to the bridge because of increasing dangers in passing through the ford.

In the 1950s the Astolat Tea Rooms, next to The Lion Hotel, was just one of many tea rooms situated in the town. Afternoon tea was a formal affair with sandwiches and cakes. Youngsters much preferred 'Joe Lyons' further up the High Street, because you could sit and chat for an hour with just one cup of tea.

In 1957 the Lion Hotel was demolished to make way for a new Woolworth's Store. This building did not survive for long and was itself replaced by White Lion Walk which opened in 1986.

This was upper High Street in 1950 with Weir Rhodes, gentlemen's tailors and outfitters, next door to Guildford House Galleries. In 1959 the Gallery moved to Nuthall's Restaurant building in the High Street. Massey, the chemist, is on the corner of North Street.

The Boxing Day hunt, which was a regular event for many years, seen here passing down the High Street on the way to Pewley Downs.

Allen House in upper High Street originally stood back from the road with a small front garden, which can just be seen on the right of this 1959 photograph.

The proximity of Allen House's front door allows us to appreciate how narrow the road was before the demolition of these upper High Street shops. Allen House did not survive as both the house and land were acquired for new Royal Grammar School building.

The Gould family lived and ran their antique business in Sussex House, upper High Street, through the 1950s until early 1960s. The house and other buildings in the group were then demolished.

The row of shops and flats were removed for road widening and this ugly building was erected in their place beside the council offices. It remained until the 1990s when thankfully it was removed; unfortunately the same fate befell the council offices.

The new development is much more pleasing to the eye and has improved this part of upper High Street.

This single-storey building in upper High Street will evoke a few memories for the older generation. At the time of this 1960 photograph it was Guildford's main library. It will also be remembered for the time, during the 1940s, when it was the Ministry of Food's British Restaurant.

In the early 1960s these buildings, belonging to Alfred Bull, marquee contractors, were the chosen site for a new library in North Street.

On the left of this group of old buildings is no 243 High Street, a property which has had a variety of uses. In 1957, Tily & Brown, ironmongers, were in residence. The District Bank then took over for a few years and by 1965 it had become a branch of the Westminster Bank. Today it is a Pizza Express outlet.

This 1975 picture shows the time when cars were sold in the High Street, from E.J. Baker's showroom. Baker's garage and workshop were situated behind Howard Morley & Sons' office building.

Today it is the Auberge Restaurant and also the entrance to Zizzi, another restaurant, on the first floor.

# London Road/Epsom Road

In 1957, at the junction of Epsom Road and London Road, a little man in his Tudor costume stood above the clock striking his bell. Where or when he went, nobody seems to know.

In this picture of Epsom Road, taken in 1975, the little man and his bell are certainly missing. The Odeon was proudly advertising its three screens, a fairly new innovation at that time. With the 1990s opening of a new multi-screen Odeon, in Bedford Road, our much-lamented old Odeon closed (*see Days of Leisure*).

# Farnham Road car-park

Guildford's engine shed, complete with turntable, occupied this site up until the late 1960s when it became Farnham Road car-park. This picture shows the car-park with its chalk face backdrop in 1987.

By 1990 the Farnham Road multi-storey car-park had replaced the open site.

# Guildford Railway Station

Guildford's Victorian railway station opened in 1845. When this photograph (above) was taken in 1977, the booking hall and offices in the main building had been out of use for many years. It was demolished in 1998, to make way for the new Guildford railway station (below).

# Burpham

Looking towards Burpham in 1984 from Clay Lane bridge, which crosses the A3. Once a rural setting, today the cows have been replaced by cars in Sainsbury's car-park.

Carry on along London Road towards Guildford to AA roundabout, where the Automobile Association had been in residence in the Fanum House building since 1934. It was a handy place to visit to collect maps and holiday information. Today the roundabout is still referred to as AA roundabout, although in 1984 they moved to a shop in Friary Street which finally closed during the 1990s.

## Stoke

Woking Road junction with Ladymead has changed a few times over the years. With the centre of the roundabout reduced in size during the 1980s, confusion resulted with lane positions. Circles were then painted to help ease the situation but this just caused even more confusion.

Now we have traffic lights and everyone waits patiently!

# Woodbridge Hill

Work started on cutting through the bank, under the railway line at Woodbridge Hill in 1976. This was a first step towards the construction of the A3 Ladymead to Burpham diversion project. Because of delays, work on the four-mile route did not begin until 1978.

The new road opened in 1981 and the Woodbridge Hill and Midleton Road junction closed. This cut off the Wooden Bridge Hotel from passing trade. For many years the hotel was a favourite stop for coaches on their way home from the coast.

# Midleton Road

To make way for the A3 diversion, 59 properties were demolished including these Midleton Road houses shown here in 1968.

A picture of Midleton Road and the A3 today, looking from the opposite direction. It shows the area between the carriageways where 29 of these houses once stood.

# Woodbridge Road

This *c.*1938 photograph shows the official opening of a section of dual carriageway in Woodbridge Road between Dapdune Road and Church Road. The ceremony was performed by the Mayor of Guildford, Robert H. Tribe (right), of the building firm Tribe and Robertson.

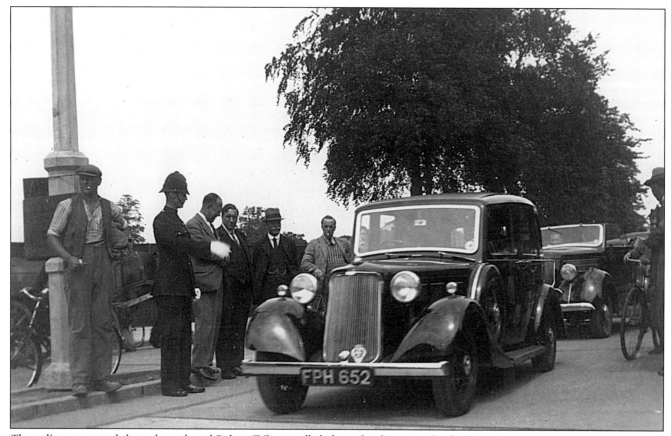

The policeman waved them through and Robert Tribe travelled along the short stretch of road in his own private, chauffeur-driven car.

Two old firms, shown here in Woodbridge Road in 1962, will be remembered by many people. Pascalls for their cycles and motorcycles, and Fogwills, who not only sold seeds and potatoes but also delivered coal and corn. They also sold and repaired lawn mowers.

The other end of Woodbridge Road in 1986, showing the Alder Valley (previously Aldershot and District) bus garage, now the site of Magnet. The Bridge Café is just visible behind the bus. Today this is the entrance to Ladymead Europa Retail Park.

On the corner of Woodbridge Road and North Street, Pascall's had another shop that not only sold bicycles but also household electrical appliances. For many years Smart's, gentlemen's hairdressers, occupied rooms above the bicycle shop.

With a decision for the redevelopment of this area still not settled, the buildings that are left in 2001 await their fate.

# *Besides the River Wey*

The River Wey has been one of the town's greatest assets. It is possible that there were settlers here 1,500 years ago and they may have lived beside the river. Guildford owes much to the Wey Navigation, founded by Sir Richard Weston of Sutton Place in 1651. Twelve locks were constructed from Guildford to Weybridge. It is thought that the Wey Navigation was the first to be provided with locks in England, with Stoke Lock being the oldest.

Town Mill and Yvonne Arnaud Theatre in 1975.

Sutton Place was built during the years 1521-6 by Sir Richard Weston, who was a favourite courtier to Henry VIII. The king was a frequent visitor to the house and it was there that he first met Anne Boleyn. Sir Richard was the great-grandfather of the founder of the Wey Navigation System, who was also named Richard. Work on the Navigation system was completed in 1653 and the estimated cost, which included digging of some 10 miles of artificial channel, was £15,000. This proved to be over-optimistic. Richard Weston died before the work finished and his son, George, was left to face mounting debts. With the prolific movement of goods both upstream and downstream, the Wey Navigation became a great success until arrival of the railway in the 19th century.

Steven's Wharf with its treadwheel shed and lifting gear pictured in 1964. The 1913 electricity works is in the background. The Stevens family had a long and close connection with the river, from three all named William Stevens dating from 1812 up until Harry Stevens who in 1963 presented navigation to the National Trust. Guildford Wharf, where barges loaded and unloaded, has long gone but the restored treadwheel is still at the site of the old wharf.

The treadwheel in 1965 in its original position at Stevens Wharf. With London barges waiting, it was here that men laboured to unload coal, one of the main cargoes brought upstream. Timber, corn and agricultural products were then loaded to be carried downstream. The last time men had to tread the wheel was in 1908.

The treadwheel in 2001, in prime position on Guildford Wharf but with no barges to service.

The National Trust has *Reliance*, an original Wey barge, on dry land at Dapdune Wharf. It was returned to Guildford in 1989, to the site where it was built in 1931-2. The *Reliance* was towed from the Essex coast by sea, up the Rivers Thames and Wey to Dapdune Wharf, where it was restored to its former condition.

Stoke Lock in the early 1900s.

Stoke Lock in 2001.

Unloading grain for the Town Mill *c.*1890. The Wey barge has just enough room to tie-up alongside. A hoist lifted the sacks to the top floor, from where grain was fed down to millstones and ground into flour.

A photograph of the Mill taken in 1964, from a position where the Yvonne Arnaud Theatre stands today.

The small building at the bottom of Rosemary Alley was converted into the Guildford Corporation mortuary in 1904. At the time of its demolition, in the early 1960s, it had not been used as a mortuary for many years.

The Guildford School of Acting now occupies the site.

*Above and below:* In the early 1900s, Millmead was a small, quiet community with cottages situated beside the river.

John Moon & Son Ltd, timber and builders' merchants, sold their site by the river in 1964 and moved to new premises in Walnut Tree Close. High Street shops adjacent to the Town Bridge and all of Moon's offices and stores were demolished. Plummer's store was erected in 1966 and it was not long before the river caused damage when the basement was flooded in 1968. The name of the store changed to Debenhams in 1972.

The wood store in this 1964 picture is the position now occupied, in 2002, by Debenhams restaurant.

Young willow trees stand alone and almost unnoticed beside the river at Millmead in this late 1950s photograph.

In 1970 the trees are starting to mature. Bridge House can be seen on the sky line and the White House is still offices. A footbridge over the river connects the two bus stations.

January 2002 and the willows dominate an area near the Town Bridge. In summertime they are a pleasant sight overhanging the river. Out of view is a new Bridge House built in 1989. The footbridge has been replaced by Friary Bridge, part of the infamous gyratory system. The offices are now the White House pub.

This scene from the 1970s has not changed very much. You can still have a cup of tea on the terrace at Debenhams or just sit on the river bank with a friend.

Alas, here is a sight rarely seen today. A pleasant scene in 1970 with ten swans grouped together on the river.

Wood from this timber yard in Millmead was swept away in the 1900 floods and helped demolish the Town Bridge (*see Against the Elements*).

In September 1999, Lampard & Partners embarked on the Riverside Apartments project in Millbrook, on the site of Martin's Garage. This involved cutting back the chalk face and erecting a 10.5 metre-high retaining wall before work could start on the 10 apartments and one house.

Riverside, Millbrook, completed in 2001.

A view from the Riverside penthouse, taken in 2000, before alterations to the Jolly Farmer public house and its change of name to The Weyside. Many other local pubs have seen their names changed over the years.

The town mill, above, at Millmead in 1964. It was built in 1771 and flour was milled here until 1894. For many years thereafter it was a waterworks for the town. The Yvonne Arnaud Theatre, pictured below, used it for a scenery workshop until it was taken over by the Mill Studio Theatre.

# Against the Elements

Unfortunately the River Wey can cause problems. It has flooded and caused damage many times over the years, notably in 1900 when the Town Bridge collapsed as timber carried downstream by floodwater wedged under the arches. The new bridge was officially opened on 5 February 1902 by the Mayor of Guildford, Mr Asher, following a procession from the Guildhall of Corporation and County Council members. Lunch was held afterwards at the County and Borough Halls at a price of 3s 6d per head (18p). Other floods were recorded in 1906, 1925, 1928, 1954, 1968, 1974, 1980, 1990, and in both January and November 2000.

The 1900 floods with St Nicolas's Church under water and, on the left, the Greyhound public house with the Connaught Hotel also suffering damage.

Same place, same problem, different year. This was the flood of 1968. The Connaught Hotel has gone and in its place was the Farnham Road bus station.

Father Goddard, the parish priest at St Nicolas's Church in 1968, manages a smile for the camera even though he had a great amount of clearing up to do in the church, including the Loseley Chapel.

This shows the main route out of town to Godalming during floods, which was via the Mount.

Residents in Leas Road, Mary Road and Walnut Tree Close had the problem of floodwater in their homes in 1968.

Although the floods caused misery to many, these youngsters found the out-of-action bus station was a great place to have some fun.

The junction of Portsmouth Road and High Street showing floodwater closing estate agents Philip & Co at no 1 and Gascoigne-Pees at no 2 High Street with Chris, gentlemen's hairdressers in Park Street, also affected.

Park Street's old Technical College building was the forerunner of Guildford College, which in 1939 opened as the Technical College in Stoke Park.

The Town Bridge was virtually covered when this lifeboat did its rounds in 1968.

This mother and daughter had trouble reaching the footbridge from Friary Square to Farnham Road bus station in 1968.

Good old 'Tracko'! Aldershot and District Traction Company in Onslow Street making an effort to carry on a service during the 1968 floods. For years, Guildford had a wonderful service from the local companies Tracko, Yellow Buses and Safeguard. There are special memories of the Yellow Buses, with stories of drivers waiting at stops knowing that a regular traveller was late. Also, the last bus from Guildford would have more passengers standing than were sitting down. The Yellow Bus Service was taken over by Aldershot and District in 1958.

Onslow Street in 1968 with the gas works buildings, Jackson's garage, D. Taylor & Son's corn merchants, and the only buildings in the picture that remain today, Seven Corners Press (Bar Mambo) and The Plaza (The Drink).

The tide's coming in at the junction of Midleton Road and Deerbarn Road, but this time it is the drains that cannot cope with the downpour. The bend in the road is the only recognisable part of this 1968 photograph. The Dennis roundabout occupies this spot today and the A3 carriageway has replaced the houses.

In 1968 Weyside Road was a through-road from Ladymead to Stoughton Road. For many years, up until 1958, it was used by the Yellow Bus Service on their route from Guildford to Bellfields. In 1976-7, eight houses and the snack bar were demolished to make way for the A3 diversion and Weyside Road became a cul-de-sac.

Outside the Wooden Bridge Hotel, a car is stranded and a taxi tries to make its way up Woodbridge Hill or Manor Road. Dennis Bros factory buildings can be seen through the trees.

In the floods of 1990, Alice would have had trouble following the White Rabbit down into its burrow to Wonderland.

November 2000 and as in the past, floodwater caused damage to the public house now known as the George Abbot.

In November 2000 the floods were the highest since 1968, nearly reaching the underside of the Town Bridge.

In contrast, this 2001 photograph shows the normal water level.

The Big Freeze of 1962-3 started with a heavy snowfall on Boxing Day 1962 and the sub-zero temperatures lasted until early March 1963. Snow and ice brought chaos to the High Street, bringing traffic to a standstill, with cars taking over an hour to negotiate the hill. Police with shovels and shop assistants with bags and sacks helped the motorist out of their plight.

*Above:* The winter of 1962-3 saw ice forming on the River Wey, but not thick enough to skate on. *Below:* But in 1895 the river at Millmead was completely frozen over. In this posed picture it looks as though a few people are wearing skates. Town Mill can be seen on the left and Quarry Street backs on the right.

Guildford City Football Club's ground at Joseph Road in January 1963. Matches were postponed for many weeks because of bad weather conditions, and the season was extended into early summer. In 1974, the ground was sold for use as building land. Langley Close now occupies the site; it is named after Jim Langley, a fine Guildford City player of the 1950s. He moved to Fulham and while he was with that club, played three times for England in 1958.

Grammar School boys enjoy the snow and ice as they make a slide outside the school.

Snow compacted on the road side and remained there for many weeks. This old bus in Rydes Avenue was probably being used to deliver groceries.

This shows the conditions in Park Road during the awful winter of 1962-3.

A picturesque scene at the AA roundabout.

Wildlife suffered during the long cold spell. These swans were grateful for the food given to them by a friendly passer-by on the river bank near old electricity works, now the Electric Theatre.

The storm in October 1987 caused havoc throughout the South-East and Guildford was not without its share of uprooted trees and blocked roads. These were the scenes in Stoke Park's Peacock Wood.

# Cathedral and University

The site for Guildford Cathedral, on Stag Hill, was donated by the fifth Earl of Onslow. The foundation stone was laid by the Archbishop of Canterbury on 22 July 1936. In 1939 building work ceased and did not resume until after the war.

The Hon Richard Bedford, Viscount Bennett, Prime Minister of Canada 1930-5, purchased land surrounding the cathedral and donated it to the diocese to commemorate the close ties between Canada and the Diocese of Guildford during World War One. Viscount Bennett emigrated to the UK in 1938 and died in 1947. He was buried in Mickleham Churchyard, Surrey, the only Canadian prime minister not to be laid to rest in Canadian soil.

Thousands of Canadian soldiers were stationed in the area then, and troops were also here during World War Two. In 1952 an appeal by the Archbishop of Canterbury brought the project to life again. One successful idea for raising funds, was for the public to purchase and sign a brick for 2s 6d (12½p). One brick even bears the Queen's signature. Gradually over the years the 'Cathedral on the Hill' took shape.

The consecration of Guildford Cathedral on 17 May 1961 was performed by Bishop Reindorp, Bishop of Guildford, in the presence of the Queen. It took a few more years before the tower and garths were completed in 1965.

The Queen and Prince Phillip sign bricks during their visit to Guildford Cathedral in 1957. Their bricks can be seen in St Ursula's Porch which is at east end of the cathedral.

A 1950s view of the foundations for the nave pillars.

The final stages of the nave being built in 1960. At the west end are three agricultural arches which were constructed to represent agricultural industry in Surrey. The notice reads, 'Visitors are invited to give their bricks for the nave now. This is your chance to share in an historic event.'

Covered scaffolding was erected in 1960 to enable Dove Brothers, the builders, to carry on working even in the worst weather. The 75ft-high by 74ft-wide scaffolding comprised 2,000 sheets of iron and at the time was one of the largest of its kind in the country.

The south view of the cathedral in 1962 with the nave finished and the tower still to be completed.

A 1963 aerial photograph looking across Onslow Village to the 'Cathedral on the Hill'.

The Angel, pointing the way in 1963.

On 4 March 1963 the 16ft tall copper Angel was placed on top of the cathedral. A cover was erected over the Angel to enable workmen to apply the gold leaf. The figure was handbeaten and made by Hurst, Franklin & Co Ltd. The Angel, which is also a weathervane, is supported on a pedestal held by a 50ft shaft and it will turn with the wind, having been mounted on ball bearings. It is known as The Golden Angel of Guildford and is in a modern classical style. The idea was conceived by Sir Edward Maufe, the cathedral architect, and designed by Mr Alan Collins. Its right arm is outstretched with a pointing finger, symbolic of a reminder to come and worship. A sheaf of lilies is carried in the left hand and the wings rise above the Angel's head. It weighs nearly a ton and was given to the cathedral by two Guildford residents, Mr and Mrs W.H. Adgey-Edgar, in memory of their eldest son who died in World War Two.

When entering Guildford Cathedral, the overriding impression is one of peace and tranquillity. The pale Somerset sandstone pillars and white Italian marble floor give a wonderful feeling of space and lightness within the building. Guildford should be proud of its 'modern' cathedral which is the first Anglican cathedral to be built on a new site in the south of England since the Reformation.

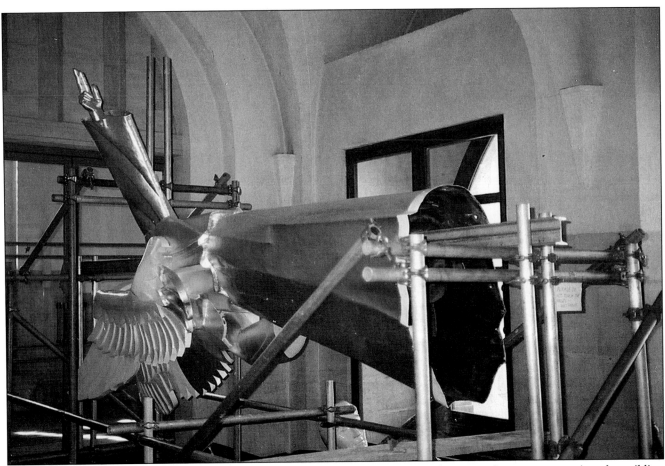

Mercury One 2 One, who have a telephone mast running up inside the Angel, paid nearly £20,000 for necessary repair and reguilding work carried out in July 2000. The Angel was removed to the west entrance of the cathedral where, in full view of visiting public, the 22-carat gold leaf was re-applied.

By September 2000 the Golden Angel of Guildford was back in its prominent position overlooking the town, still pointing the way.

Guildford Cathedral stands alone on Stag Hill in 1965. When in the early 1960s it was decided that the University of Surrey was to be built on Stag Hill, there was a certain amount of alarm amongst the natives. All those long-haired students descending on our quiet town! In 1968 the first students arrived and there was still strong resentment over the presence of the university. As the years have passed it has grown and become integrated into the community. Now you cannot imagine Guildford without its university.

Today as you view the cathedral from a similar position as in 1965, it no longer seems so remote from the town. The university now forms a link between the two. When travelling back to Guildford at night, there can be a warm feeling inside when you first see the cathedral illuminated on Stag Hill. You know that you will soon be home.

The university blends in well with the earlier-built cathedral, and the landscaped gardens provide a tranquil setting within the campus for students and staff.

The modern Duke of Kent Building at the university sits at the foot of Stag Hill, facing the town. It won the award presented by the Guildford Society for best new building design in 2000.

# Tending the Sick

Number 53 Quarry Street, at the junction with Castle Street, pictured here in 1965 when it was a newsagent's shop, has a very interesting history. At one time it was the forerunner of the Royal Surrey County Hospital. It started life in 1745 as a beer house the Kitt, which was renamed the Sheep Shearer's. Then it changed to the King's Head and afterwards became the Sun public house. It was also a butcher's shop and a bakery.

Then in 1859 a group of private individuals met in the White Hart Hotel in the High Street and planned to open a dispensary for the relief of the sick and poor of the town and neighbourhood. On 2 January 1860, the Guildford Dispensary, later called the West Surrey Dispensary, opened in the building. It provided medical and surgical outpatients' facilities and also some home visiting. In its first year 1,185 patients were seen, of whom 475 were visited in their homes. When the Royal Surrey County Hospital in Farnham Road opened in 1866, the dispensary closed and the premises became the Sun public house again.

After the Sun closed in 1894, various shops occupied the building, including a cycle shop, tobacconist's and in the 1960s, Bridleways, the saddlers, who stayed until 1985. By this time the building was in a sorry state. The council purchased the property in 1962 and had plans to demolish it so that Castle Street could be widened. Thankfully these plans were shelved and restoration work was carried out in 1987.

Across the field, which today is the site of Guildford County School, we see the Royal Surrey County Hospital as it was in 1865 with the Hillier Almshouses to its left. Note the numerous chimney stacks protruding from the hospital roof. It is hard to imagine all the smoke and dust that must have made its way into the wards when fires were lit during wintertime.

The six-plus acres of land needed for the hospital in Farnham Road were donated by Lord Onslow. The foundation stone was laid in July 1863 and the hospital opened its doors to patients on 27 April 1866 with 60 beds. It was named the Royal Surrey County Hospital, with the approval of Queen Victoria, in memory of her consort, Prince Albert. In 1948 the hospital was handed over to the NHS and as a result of an extension and new buildings the number of beds was increased to 228.

Edward Ward, with its 20 beds plus ten beds in an enclosed balcony, was placed at the disposal of the War Office for use during World War One. The first wounded soldiers arrived via Guildford railway station on 15 October 1914 and continued up until 1917; altogether some 556 patients were received into Edward Ward.

Soon after the war started, it was realised that more beds would be required. The County School, which had just been built opposite the hospital, was converted and staffed by the Guildford Division of the Red Cross and used as a 102-bed annex to the RSCH.

The first soldiers arrived on 12 January 1915 and by the end of 1918, a total of 2,730 patients had been treated in the annex. However, the largest and most important Guildford Hospital during World War One was Warren Road Military Hospital, later St Luke's Hospital.

Above is shown the Warren Road Military War Hospital. The St Luke's Hospital site originally started as the Guildford Union Workhouse. The six and a half acres of land were purchased in February 1837 for £150 per acre and the workhouse opened in 1838. It was early in 1916 that the Union Workhouse and Infirmary were utilised for sick and wounded from the war. Up until August 1919, some 7,680 patients had passed through the wards. In 1938 the buildings were designated as a general hospital and renamed Warren Road Hospital, and then to St Luke's in 1945.

The archway entrance to the Union Workhouse, facing Cooper Road, was demolished in 1965.

The Casual Ward at the workhouse, known as the Spike, opened in 1905 to provide tramps with overnight accommodation, a bath and a hot meal. They were locked up for the night in their rooms (really more like cells), then made to leave next day. The old Spike is the only building that remains from the Union Workhouse and St Luke's Hospital and the building has now been placed under a preservation order.

The spy holes allowed no privacy for inmates; it was just like being in a prison cell. Some of the graffiti is dated 1906.

Four of the tiny rooms had doors to a work area for breaking stones which had to be small enough to pass through a grill, as shown here. This was punishment for troublesome inmates, or men that called at the Spike too often. The stones were sold to help with the expenses of running the Spike.

The World War One 'Soldiers' Cemetery' at Stoughton.

Although doctors and nurses worked tirelessly, many of the soldiers died of their wounds or from illness. They were generally conveyed to their home towns or villages for burial. However, over 70 of those who died in Guildford hospitals lie in Stoughton Cemetery, most of them in the 'Soldiers' Cemetery' facing a memorial cross.

One woman, Staff Nurse Elizabeth Annie Challinor of the Queen Alexandra Imperial Nursing Service, who died in 1918, aged 29, is also buried there near the memorial cross. Elizabeth Annie was in fact from Guildford. Her home was in Caxton Gardens, Stoughton. Military honours were accorded to the fallen heroes. The band of The Queen's Regiment, stationed at Stoughton Barracks, generally attended the funerals.

Remembering that Guildford was a much smaller town in those days, it shows the magnitude of lives lost in World War One, when the Borough of Guildford lost 493 of its young men in the conflict. There were few roads in Guildford that were not affected, losing at least one of their menfolk. For every man that died, it was thought another dozen were wounded, and many suffered with their experiences for the rest of their lives. The sadness of it all is shown in the tragedy suffered by my old friend Reg Collier's grandparents, Mr and Mrs W. Collier of Springfield Road, who lost three sons, two in 1915 and one in 1917.

Elizabeth Annie Challinor's gravestone.

139

World War Two saw the Royal Surrey County Hospital utilised once again for the war effort. Dr Heward Bell, a physician there during that time, remembers the call to move all patients from the hospital and prepare for the D-Day landing casualties as RSCH was to be a clearing station. Convoys of ambulances arrived at 1am with the first casualties and doctors and nurses worked continuously until 8am. They then went off and attended to their general patients who had been moved to Merrow Grange and Puttenham Priory. Dr Bell recalls getting very little sleep during a 10-day period.

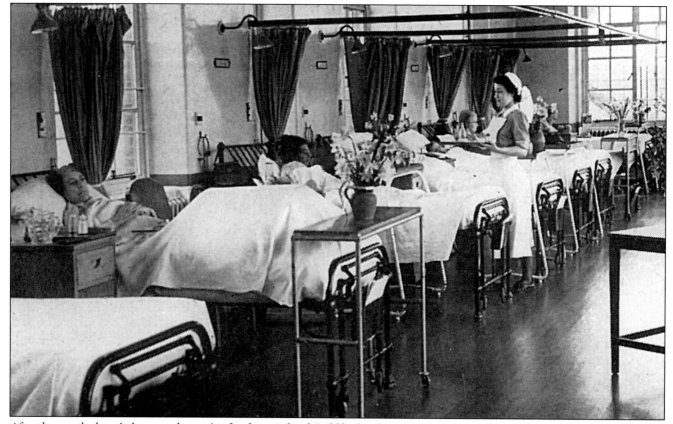

After the war the hospital returned to caring for the people of Guildford and surrounding districts only. This photograph, taken in the early 1950s, shows Victoria Ward which probably had about 20 beds.

The Queen and Prince Philip visited the Royal Surrey County Hospital in June 1957 when they came to the town to commemorate the anniversary of the Royal Charter granted to the Borough of Guildford.

Nurses are seen relaxing in their sitting room at the RSCH. In 1957 nurses could look forward to a salary structure which today is difficult to comprehend. First-year student nurses earned £260 per annum, rising to £285 in their third and final year. Unfortunately £119 was deducted from this sum to pay for board and lodging.

Work on the first phase of the new Guildford District General Hospital started in January 1972. It was planned to complete all three phases during the 1980s. Serious economic problems prevented the construction work to phase one from being completed until 1979. On 27 February 1981, The Queen officially opened the East Wing and named it The Royal Surrey County Hospital.

It was not until September 1991 that phase two, called the West Wing, was officially opened by the Duke of Kent. After much delay phase three, the St Luke's Wing, was finally opened on 21 February 1997 by The Queen, patron of the RSCH. This followed the transfer of services from the old St Luke's Hospital in Warren Road.

The old Royal Surrey County Hospital in Farnham Road served the community of south-west Surrey for just over 113 years. It may sound odd to say that one has fond memories of a hospital, but it trained some wonderful nurses. It is now called the Farnham Road Hospital.

# *Time Gentlemen Please...*

Many public houses have closed in Guildford during the last 40 years. This photograph shows the Castle Inn at bottom of Farnham Road in 1974. It was demolished in 1986.

The Bear in Friary Street was one of Guildford's oldest public houses. Part of the front elevation of this 16th-century building remained after its demolition in 1967. It was incorporated into the new buildings in Friary Street, which became a pedestrian area. It is a small reminder of the Bear, in a street that was once known as Bear Lane.

*Above:* The Railway Hotel, situated on the corner of Bridge Street and lower Farnham Road, during its demolition in 1963 for road improvements. *Below:* The same corner in 2001.

The Prince of Wales stood next to St Saviour's Church in Woodbridge Road for over 100 years until the site was redeveloped in 1972. The photograph below was taken in 2001.

This photograph of the Seven Stars in Swan Lane was taken in 1973, one year before it was badly damaged by an IRA bomb on Saturday 5 October 1974. Fifteen people were injured, including landlord Brian Owen O'Brien and his wife Dorothy. Mr O'Brien heard the blast which occurred at the Horse and Groom in North Street and went to see what had happened. After seeing the damage he rushed back to tell everyone to leave his pub. His quick action undoubtedly saved more people from being injured. The pub reopened in April 1975 after £10,000 was spent on repairing the building and £12,000 on alterations and refurbishment to the interior, Unfortunately not long afterwards it closed for good.

The building is once again being used to provide refreshments, only now instead of beer it is fruit juice and coffee.

This pub started life as the Emperor Napoleon III Hotel in 1855 but by the time the top photograph was taken in 1973 it had changed from Napoleon III to just Napoleon. It closed in 1978 and remained empty for many years until an office development, shown below in 1990, was built.

An early 1900s photograph of the Bull's Head with the Red Lion Hotel on other side of Market Street.

The demise of the Bull's Head, which was situated in the centre of Guildford High Street, was a sad loss of an extremely popular public house. The building originated in *c.*1550. Whether it was an ale house from the start is not known. The earliest mention of the inn was in 1625.

Since Victorian times it has been known as the Bull's Head but previously it was called the Bull Head. The first mention of the changed name appeared in 1826 and at the same time it was also known as the New Bull's Head. Considerable alterations were carried out, probably in the 18th century, when the building was divided into two properties. By the early 1950s the now-listed building was showing its age and needed a tremendous amount of repair work to make it safe. Because of the constant vibration from heavy traffic using Market Street and pressure on the building from adjacent properties located up the hill the Bull's Head was leaning towards Market Street. Whitbread & Co Ltd, the owners at that time, took on task of restoration in 1955 and pub re-opened in 1956.

All went well until 1972 when the real saga of the Bull's Head began. An application from Whitbreads to convert the building into a shop was refused, first by Guildford Borough Council then by Surrey South-West Planning Sub-Committee who had received a petition from 1,651 Bull's Head customers.

The Bull's Head in 1955 before work had started on restoration of the building. The plumb line shows how far it was tilting towards Market Street. Note also the midday papers for sale on the pavement. You left your money and took your paper. Those were the days!

General agreement was that the Bull's Head was an integral part of a group of buildings including the Guildhall. Any conversion to a shop would be a loss to local amenities and out of character with the group of buildings. By July 1973, Whitbreads had sold the property and with it a new threat of closure arose. The new owners, Corinth Investment Holdings Ltd, applied for change of use to a restaurant.

A petition with 11,396 signatures was accepted by the Mayor, Mr B. Bellerby before a Guildford Borough Council meeting. The pub stayed empty and vandals broke windows and the signs were painted over.

The first job to be carried out, during the 1950s restoration was to erect shoring to give support to side wall which appeared in danger of collapse. Flying shores were fixed to the walls of Timothy White's building, across the road.

A view of the bar looking towards the High Street during restoration. The entrance is in the far right-hand corner.

With the restoration completed the Bull's Head was ready for customers in 1956. Although the bar was only small, it had plenty of character.

The restaurant overlooking the High Street was a popular place to eat.

In April 1974 there were calls for a compulsory purchase order to be placed on the pub. People had strong feelings about the Bull's Head, however, and in August the same year an attempt was made to set up a trust to purchase the pub. The problem was that Corinth Investment Holdings were thought to have paid £250,000 and would most certainly want more than that for the building.

In July 1975, Whitbreads were reported to be interested in buying back the pub, but by January 1976 estate agents had failed to let or sell the property and it was taken off the market. In August businessmen Messrs Stearn and Riley bought the property for 'very much less' than £250,000 and in October that year Guildford's oldest pub reopened.

For 12 years the Bull's Head continued to be a favourite meeting place but in May 1988 the property was sold to Victory Land. The price was believed to be £1,250,000. Victory Land said they intended to refurbish the pub and let it 'to the best people'. A brewery was not ruled out. Alas, the Bull's Head closed once more on 20 May 1988 and an announcement from the Department of the Environment in 1989, allowing pubs to be converted into shops without planning permission, paved the way for the Bull's Head to be changed to retail premises.

The next few pages show photographs of five Guildford hotels or inns which were part of the town scene in early 1900. The Ram Inn on the corner of High Street and Chertsey Street was demolished in 1913 to give extra width to the High Street and to enable easier access into Chertsey and North Streets.

The same corner in 1973 with the Barclays Bank building illustrating the easier curve to the road which is now the junction between High Street and North Street.

One of the High Street coaching inns, the White Lion Hotel, later named the Lion Hotel, survived until 1957. The Half Moon public house on the left was demolished in 1900.

In this 1956 picture, notice the extension to the hotel, where the entrance has been moved downhill on to the site of the Half Moon.

The Friary Brewery Tap was situated on the corner of North Street and Swan Lane. It was formerly known as the Coachmaker's Arms, a 19th-century beerhouse which had a poor reputation in the town. The Friary Brewery Tap closed in 1911.

Various retail outlets have occupied the building over the years. In 1973 it was Bernard's the butcher, who also had a grocery store further up North Street with an entrance in High Street.

The Crown, which adjoined Abbot's School in North Street, was originally used as a workhouse for the poor people of local parishes. In about 1867 it opened as a beer house. The building projected into North Street, reducing the carriageway to 15ft. It survived until 1907 and was then demolished when it became necessary to widen the road.

This was how the same location looked in 1973; it still looks very similar today. If you walk up North Street and look up at the end wall of the old Abbot School building you can still see the roof line of the Crown Inn.

The Barley Mow Inn was on corner of the Mount and Park Street. In the early 1800s the pub's stables probably supplied extra horses to help coaches climb the Mount when it was a main route out of town to Farnham. By 1908 the inn had closed.

The same corner in 1974, showing the Park Street salon of Chris, gentlemen's hairdressers, At this time he also ran a unisex salon in Lea Pale Road.

The last few years have seen name changes to many public houses in Guildford. The Carpenter's Arms, Leapale Road, shown above in 1975, became the Mary Rose in 1982 (below) and, more recently, the Five and Lime in 2000.

Five and Lime, now there is an interesting name for a pub. It has always been the case that pubs have changed their names over the centuries. But Carpenter's Arms to Five and Lime? What does it mean?

For over 100 years the public house situated at the end of Stoke Fields was called the Elm Tree. In the 1990s it was renamed the Tap and Spile. Thankfully, it has now reverted to the Elm Tree.

The Drummond Arms, Woodbridge Road, in 1973 with a shop situated next door.

It is now the Forger and Firkin with the shop turned into a brewing room.

Since the mid-19th century the name Britannia had been associated with this site, either as a beer house or public house. That is until Scruffy Murphys arrived in the 1990s.

The Greyhound in lower High Street in 1973. At least the name change to George Abbot has an association with Guildford.

The Foresters Arms (above) in Cline Road as it was in 1974. The pub's name has changed a few times from the Forester in 1870 to the Forester Inn in 1871 and then to the Forester Arms in 1944. For many years it was known locally as the Pig and Tater. The owners then bowed to the inevitable and in 1976 that became its official name. Guess what, though? It is now named Forresters (below).

The Cannon in Portsmouth Road was originally part of the Cannon Brewery which was built on the site between lower Portsmouth Road and Bury Street in 1844. Also shown in this 1974 picture is Jackson's cycle shop with the Central Electricity Generating Board offices on the right.

Everything has changed in 2001. Jackson's was demolished many years ago and the Power House which replaced the Cannon is now next to an empty site due to the recent demolition of the CEGB building. This has opened up a view of the 1838 Caleb Lovejoy Armshouses in Bury Street.

The Green Man public house at Burpham converted to a Harvester pub and restaurant in 1984. In the early 1960s, when it was a main stopover for coach parties from London on their way to the coast, Brian and Sylvia Wheeler became the licensees and remained there until 1984. They recall the time when 28 coaches were packed into the car-park. Unfortunately, sometimes they had trouble keeping their glasses because many customers wanted to keep them as souvenirs. On one occasion they had a police escort along the A3 to reclaim the missing glasses from London-bound coaches.

A photograph of the Green Man taken from Pantile's garage in the 1930s.

The Stoke Hotel, seen above in 1975, was converted from a large house to a licenced property in 1870. Renovation work was carried out in 1989 and the name changed to Finnegan's Wake (below) in the 1990s.

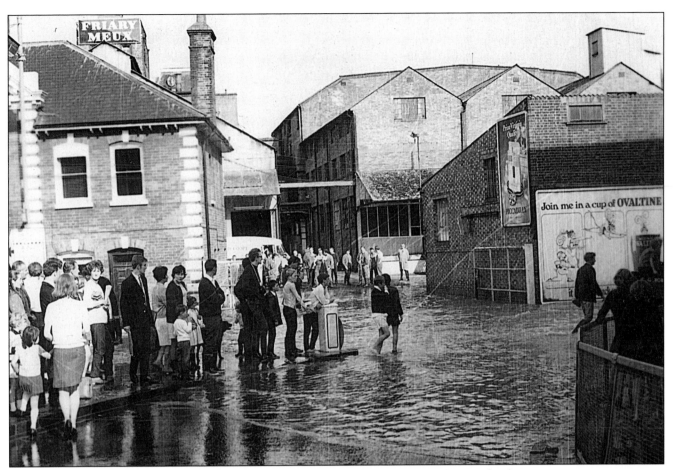

The Friary Brewery entrance at the junction of Onslow Street and Bridge Street during the 1968 floods.

In 1969 brewing ceased at the Friary Brewery. The closure and demolition of the buildings took place in 1973-4. It was the last surviving brewery in Guildford and many will remember the smell of hops which would waft over the town at frequent intervals.

Dynamite was used to blow out the front of the Friary Tower at 4.30pm on Sunday 17 February 1974, after it had failed to do so earlier in the day.

This picture shows rubble from the tower in Commercial Road, now site of the bus station.

# *Days of Leisure*

For years the only indoor swimming pool in the town was Castle Street Baths. It was quite basic with individual changing cubicles situated along both sides of the pool. Nevertheless it was very popular, especially with youngsters. An added bonus was the deep cast-iron baths. With many houses not having bathrooms, local families were quite happy to use the baths with their constant supply of hot water, instead of tin baths in front of the living-room fire. Castle Street Baths closed in 1972 when Bedford Road Sports Centre opened.

Bedford Road Sports Centre served the people of Guildford and district for 21 years. It was built on part of the town's old gas works site and was designed to meet family sporting needs which had been sadly lacking in the town for many years. When it opened it was thought to be the finest in the south of England. The Odeon Cinema complex now occupies the site.

For many years, Guildford people who wanted to ice skate had to wait for the River Wey to freeze over, or travel to Richmond Ice Rink. Today, however, there is the popular Spectrum Leisure Centre in Stoke Park with not only an ice rink but also swimming pools, tenpin bowling, an athletics track, a gymnasium and more. Spectrum, which opened in 1993, replaced the Bedford Road Sports Centre.

Spectrum has three pools which cater for a wide range of interests. These include a teaching pool, a 25-metre pool for lane swimming, which is also used by Guildford City Swimming Club, and a leisure pool just for a having a good time.

Guildford has waited a long time for its ice rink. It has been a great success, not only for individual skaters but for ice shows, competitions and, of course, home to Guildford Flames, the town's own ice-hockey team.

Ten-pin bowling is for all ages at the Spectrum Leisure Centre.

Stoke Park must be one of the best acquisitions the Town Council has ever made. It was purchased by Guildford Corporation from H.M. Budgett in 1925 with the intention that it should be used for recreational purposes. Before this time it had been used for events such as the Royal Counties Shows, and in 1872 for a grand fête held to celebrate the anniversary of Queen Victoria's coronation,.

The Japanese-style ornamental gardens were opened in 1935 with a children's boating lake, paddling pool, lily pond and a rock garden with waterfalls. The boating lake is still a popular place for families. The bridge had major repairs in 1984 after being closed for a few years for safety reasons.

Alderman William Harvey, conscious of high unemployment in Guildford and beyond during the 1930s, started a work fund to build the Lido. Local labour and men from south Wales and the north-east, who had moved to Guildford, were employed. It proved a great success. Town residents contributed money weekly and the local council donated £3,000 to the fund. It took 600 men six months to complete the work. William Harvey became Mayor of Guildford and he opened the Lido in 1933 by diving into the pool.

On a beautiful summer's evening in June 1998, the Guildford Philharmonic Orchestra performed a selection of water music at the Lido. Many people enjoyed picnics on the lawn whilst listening to the music.

This was Stoke Mansion in the 1920s when it was a preparatory school for 'the sons of gentlemen'. An advertisement boasted, 'Home life, individual tuition, backward boys a speciality, very careful moral training'. There were also riding lessons in the park.

A photograph taken in 2001 from the same spot as the above.

Stoke Park Mansion, a fine 18th-century house, was an integral part of the park for many years. A few years before the Corporation took over the park, the mansion opened as a boarding school for boys which did not close until 1935. After this, until its demolition in 1977, the building was used as an annex to the Technical College.

For anyone who visited the house a lasting memory must be of the grand sweeping staircase, pictured here. The County Technical College and School of Art (Guildford College) was built in the park in 1937-8 and opened for students in 1939, replacing the College in Park Street.

Stoke Park caters for all ages and the playground near the Stoke Road area is well used.

Another place in the park for youngsters is the skateboard park, which is situated next to the Guildford College annex.

The paddling pool evokes fond memories for many Guildford people and with many recent improvements it is still a joy for children.

For years there was a problem with the pool leaking and it was beginning to show its age. In 1989 the council completely rebuilt the pool, adding modern filters and an automatic chlorination system. What better way for young families to spend a hot summer's afternoon than at Stoke Park paddling pool? In fact, just like the children shown here enjoying themselves in July 2001.

Guildford Model Engineering Society moved to their present site, at the London Road end of Stoke Park in 1958, from a small hut in Woking Road. The foundation stone of the pavilion was laid by Alderman Nicklin on 3 October 1959. At any one time there are generally about 200 members in the society. With the enthusiasm of past and present members over the last 40 years, all building work, track lay-out, construction and repair work to the locomotives has been carried out in-house. Every year the society has a model steam rally which attracts enthusiasts from around Britain and Europe, many bringing their caravans and staying the weekend.

There are also regular open days for the public, who can enjoy rides on the model trains with generally up to five engines on show.

Guildford Crusaders Bible Class moved to their new hall in Stoke Park in 1974. Their meetings had been held in different places around the town since the first class in 1910. Many years were spent at 5 Dapdune Crescent in Woodbridge Road. (see *The Crusaders*)

Next to the Crusaders' hall is Challengers, a play centre for disabled children and young people. The centre evolved from an idea by consultant paediatrician Dr Helen Foley, and Colin Hassell, deputy manager of the old Bedford Road Sports Centre, that disabled children should have a special place to play with their siblings and non-disabled children. In 1979, sessions for disabled children only were held at the sports centre. Over the next five years funds were raised, a site in Stoke Park acquired and the Guildford Adventurers' Play Centre was born. It was opened by Princess Margaret in 1984.

In 1994 the charity changed its name to Disability Challenge and the centre was renamed Challengers. Disability Challengers, a registered charity, provides play and leisure opportunities for children and young people with any special needs – physical, learning, sensory, emotional or social. Children and young people up to the age of 25 enjoy the activities at Challengers.

There is a wide variety of equipment, games and toys at the centre, some being very sophisticated, such as their multi-sensory unit, while others are designed and built to support children with particular impairments. Much of the equipment, however, is identical to that found in any playgroup, and whatever the children are doing, the emphasis is always for them to have fun. Disability Challengers also works to support other organisations in the community to provide inclusive play and leisure activities using mainstream facilities. It is the only charity of its kind based in this area, supporting children from all over Surrey, the surrounding counties and south London.

The aim now is to open another Challengers Centre, building on the success of the Guildford Centre.

The 18th-century Burchatt's Farm cottages and barn, opposite Challengers, are all that remain of the farm which the former Guildford Corporation acquired in 1925. When it was restored in 1989, the project won a Guildford Heritage Award.

This photograph shows the building in its early stages of restoration.

Burchatt's Farm was one of many Guildford buildings restored by Lampard and Partners.

The barn, which is owned by Guildford Borough Council, may be hired for private functions. With its original beams and brickwork it is an ideal venue for parties and receptions.

## The Crusaders

On a Saturday afternoon in November 1910, Dr Alan Pimm met with a group of boys playing football on Pewley Downs. After the game he talked about his Christian beliefs. They met on further Saturday afternoons until winter and then moved to a rented room in Leapale Road. By this time Lawrence, known as 'Guv', had joined his brother and they moved to a room over Fogwills in Friary Street.

World War One came and Alan joined the army. In 1915, 'Guv' provided and equipped an ambulance for work at the front, and took it to France where he drove it himself. During the war years, boys continued meeting and the class was kept open.

After the war 'Doc' Pimm had to leave because of work commitments so 'Guv' took over the running of the class by himself. They moved to Harvey Road, then to a house on the corner of Lea Pale Road and Lea Pale Lane and eventually to 5 Dapdune Crescent where they stayed until 1972.

When 'Guv' died in 1960, the class mourned the loss of a man who had built Guildford Crusaders into a strong and vibrant group. Guildford Crusaders is not only a Bible class but has over the years excelled in all manner of sports including football, cricket, canoeing and sailing. Each year there is a summer camp in either Cornwall or Wales, In the 1940 and '50s the camp was at Portscatho, Cornwall. The class still holds a summer camp there every third year. There must be hundreds of Guildford men who have fond memories of the Guildford Crusaders.

Guildford Crusaders in 1950. This photograph of the Junior Class was taken in the garden of 5 Dapdune Crescent, Guildford. Leaders sitting left to right are Jack Ives, Roland Jenkins and 'Guv' Pimm.

Guildford Crusaders on Portscatho beach, 'chariot racing' during the 1951 summer camp. The right-hand team had Michael Campbell-Lamerton, in the dark top, a Guildford boy who went on to play rugby for Scotland and the British Lions.

'Guv' Pimm provided a lorry, seen in this 1954 photograph, to transport kit and a few of the boys to summer camp.

The Methodist Church is the only building in this picture that is standing today. Number 5 Dapdune Crescent, Guildford Crusader's Hall, is the house next to the church. This photograph was taken in 1972 just days before these fine buildings were pulled down.

A group of Guildford teenagers at the Amsterdam Youth Hostel in 1955. Sylvia Watts, The Guildford Assistant Youth Organiser, arranged a trip to Holland in 1955 which included members from Charlotteville Youth Club and seven other clubs in the town. For most of the 58 teenagers, staying a week in the Amsterdam Youth Hostel was their first trip abroad. For many years afterwards Sylvia led trips to Holland, Austria and Italy. Many couples met on these holidays and later married.

The Stoke Hotel ballroom during a Young Conservatives dance in 1960, when men wore suits, white shirts and ties.

In the early 1960s, the Stoke Hotel was one of the main venues for Saturday night dances that were held in and around the town. After one dance organised by the Young Conservatives, the *Surrey Advertiser* reported that a group of supporters from an opposing political party attended the dance sporting red ties, proving that it was a non-political occasion. It was indeed non-political, but the red ties were part of a group identity and in fact one person always wore a blue tie and he was the leader for that evening and had to be obeyed.

Other popular venues for Saturday night dances were Onslow Village, Compton and Cranleigh Village Halls. The place you had to attend and be 'seen' was the Sandfield Terrace Drill Hall, which held regular dances with top live bands of the day including Johnny Dankworth and Cleo Lane, George Melly, Eric Delaney and Chas McDevitt with Nancy Whiskey and many more. They would all finish at midnight.

On New Year's Eve there would be an extension until 1am with tickets for this night sold out weeks in advance. Then it would be a long walk home, or if you were very lucky, a lift in one of the few cars available. Taxis were for a very special occasion.

Today it is apparently a bit different. At night clubs in town, such as The Drink, people arrive at the time we were leaving to go home. On Friday and Saturday nights Guildford has become a 'mecca' for young people to have a good time in the night clubs and bars in Bridge Street and the surrounding area. They regularly travel from other towns as far away as Portsmouth.

Sandfield Terrace Drill Hall awaiting its demolition. Thousands of Guildfordians have fond memories of this old hall. The Drink night club in Onslow Street will have the same effect on a another generation of dancers.

It is hard to imagine that this area is now home to some excellent entertainment in Guildford. The redundant electricity works building and the flooded bus station in 1968. A reminder of times past, schoolboys wear their caps and even in wet weather all have well-polished shoes. Today, as adults, some of them may revisit the area to go to the theatre.

Guildford Borough Council financed the conversion of the old electricity works into the Electric Theatre. It is also funded and managed by the same local authority. The idea was to have a venue where local amateur theatre groups could perform and in this respect it has proved a great success.

On the end wall is the date 1913. It is probably due to this that the derelict building was saved from demolition years ago. Today we know it was a wise decision, and surprising considering it was not the most attractive of buildings.

Guildford Amateur Theatre Association was set up in 1983 to lobby for a permanent home for town's amateur performing arts groups. In 2002 the Electric Theatre was home to 40 local societies who make up GATA.

The shell of the old building, ready for construction of auditorium.

The seats are in place and after a few finishing touches the theatre is ready for its opening in January 1997.

The audience is seated – let the entertainment begin. Various groups and societies use the Electric Theatre, including theatre and opera companies, singing and youth groups, dancers and film makers.

With the 210 seats fully retracted, a semi-sprung dance floor is revealed. The auditorium is available for hire and can be used for private functions, dinner-dances, barn dances, quiz nights and exhibitions.

The old Odeon building in 2002, still empty and derelict, awaiting its fate.

The Odeon opened its doors to the public for first time on Monday 13 May 1935 with Jack Buchanan in the film *Brewster's Millions*. It was advertised as 'the new luxury theatre' with 1,000 stall seats at 1s 6d (8p) for the grand opening performance. There were about 1,800 seats to start with but this was reduced after a few years to 1,200. In 1950s-60s it was an ideal venue to stage live performances. In the Big Band era, top bands played at the Odeon including Ted Heath's Band with singers Lita Rosa, Dickie Valentine and Dennis Lotus. Chris Barber was a regular visitor with his Jazz Band.

Stars such as Vera Lynn, Max Bygraves, Jimmy Edwards and even the London Festival Ballet gave performances. Pop concerts in the 1960s included Tommy Steele, the Rolling Stones, Cliff Richard, and the Beatles. In 1973 the Odeon was converted from a single screen to a three-screen cinema and seating reduced to 722. Let us hope that good use is found for this building which will benefit the town.

The Plaza Cinema closed in 1957 and reopened as a dance hall. For years up until the 1960s, Guildford had four cinemas: the Odeon in Epsom Road, the Plaza in Onslow Street, the Cinema in Woodbridge Road and the Playhouse in the High Street. The Odeon was certainly tops for comfort, with the Plaza being least comfortable of the four. If you were unlucky enough to be seated behind one of the Plaza's pillars, you spent your time leaning over the person next to you. That is, unless you were in the back row, in which case you did not watch the film anyway!

**CENTRAL HALL**

# PICTURE PALACE

## Continuous Performance

EVERY DAY  -  2.30 to 10.30.
SATURDAYS  -  2 to 10.30.

TEAS PROVIDED FREE OF CHARGE.

PRICES OF ADMISSION:

**BALCONY** -  -  -  - 6d. and 1s.
**STALLS**  - Children, 2d.; Adults, 3d.

*1/- Seats may be booked without extra charge.*

Cycles Stored, 1d.                    Telephone 368.

# ONSLOW ST., GUILDFORD.

A 1912 advertisement for the Picture Palace which was later renamed the Plaza.

The 1920s cinema building has survived into the 21st century and is now Bojangles night club. By the 1950s its name had changed to the Guildford Cinema and Café. In the 1960s it was altered to the Astor and the 1970s saw a further change when it became Studios 1 and 2.

In the 1950-60s you always seemed to queue for a long time, in all weathers, when visiting the cinema. This was not too much of a problem at the Playhouse, which had an arcade leading from the High Street. On Sundays they showed two different films to the ones screened during the week. Many people regularly went to the cinema twice a week and on Sundays they would sometimes queue without knowing which films were being shown, although at the Playhouse main feature films were usually westerns, probably starring Randolph Scott.

# Celebrations

Over the years the High Street has seen some elaborate decorations erected for special occasions. These in 1897 were to celebrate the 60th anniversary of Queen Victoria's Coronation.

The Town Bridge in 1897, decorated for Queen Victoria's Diamond Jubilee.

Part of the elaborate decorations which adorned the town to celebrate the silver jubilee of King George V's accession to the throne, was a medieval wooden arch erected in 1935 next to the Town Bridge. It greeted visitors as they crossed the river into lower High Street. The idea however was not original; a similar arch was built in 1911 in the same place for King George's Coronation. Sadly, only a few months after the May celebrations, King George V died on 20 January 1936. The population's joy was replaced by sorrow.

High Street decorations in 1953 were to commemorate the Coronation of Queen Elizabeth II. The country was still recovering from World War Two and there was hope that the Coronation would be the start of better times ahead. Many purchased their first television set especially for the occasion. All day they sat watching the ceremony at Westminster Abbey, the processions and crowds gathering outside Buckingham Palace, waiting for the Queen and other members of royal family to appear on the balcony. In at least one Guildford home there was a television set which overheated and had to be turned off.

Crowds packed the High Street in 1957 to greet the Queen when she visited the town on the 700th anniversary of Henry III granting a royal charter to the Borough of Guildford. Although Guildford has a cathedral, the town still awaits city status.

On the Guildhall balcony the Queen is presented with a plum cake from the High Steward, Lord Onslow. It is a tradition carried out when reigning monarchs visit the town on an official visit. Mayor Harold Kimber, who was in his third term of office, is standing to the Queen's left. Next to him is the recorder, Mr T. Christmas Humphreys, and Richard Nugent, MP for Guildford. 'Sam' Weller, the long-serving town clerk, is on the right.

Outside the Guildhall, the Queen inspects a guard of honour comprising soldiers from the Queen's Regiment.

Twenty years later the Bull's Head has permission to open all day for the Queen's Silver Jubilee, a rare occurrence in 1977. Guildford planned numerous events, throughout the summer, to celebrate the occasion. These included a pageant in Shalford Park, which ran for two weeks. There was also a two-day Guildford Town Show held in Stoke Park with a carnival procession through the town centre, and thanksgiving service at the cathedral, attended by the Archbishop of Canterbury.

On 9 February 2002, from the steps of Holy Trinity Church, the High Sheriff of Surrey, Bill Biddell, reads a proclamation which congratulated the Queen on the 50th anniversary of her accession to the throne. His first duty, however, was to announce the sad news that Princess Margaret had died peacefully in her sleep earlier that morning. A few weeks later, of course, Queen Elizabeth The Queen Mother also passed away peacefully.

With the Union Flag at half-mast, dignitaries and the assembled crowd were subdued, but there was still an emotional response to the request for 'three cheers for the Queen', and the National Anthem was robustly sung.

Back in September 1939, Stoughton Infant School was commandeered by the Army at the outbreak of the war. By January 1940, the children were back in school and, pictured here, in 1945 they were ready to celebrate victory. The headmistress, Miss Shrimpton, is at the back on far right-hand side.

Three years later: some of the same pupils at Stoughton Junior School.

Another class of 1948 at Stoughton Juniors with the headmaster, Mr Hardy.

With the war in Europe over it was time to have a party. This was Harts Gardens, Stoughton, in 1945, celebrating VE Day. The four cars on view were probably the full complement for a street in which there were 47 houses. The cars were used to give children a treat with trips around local roads.

Although children in Harts Gardens did not have many possessions during the war, they did have excitement because of where they lived. With Stoughton Barracks at the bottom of their gardens, a REME depot and an ATS (later Women's Royal Army Corps) camp at the end of the road, there was plenty of military activity. The worry and stress suffered by their parents did not affect local children in the same way.

After the war Stoughton was used as a demobilization centre. When the men were demobbed they travelled in lorries to Guildford railway station. It was a great opportunity, while civilians queued for lorries, to ask them for their cap badges and foreign coins. Still persistent, two or three of the boys would travel with the driver to the station hoping for better luck there.

A Stoughton VE Day party in May 1945.

Another Harts Gardens children's party, this time celebrating VJ Day in August 1945. With the surrender of the Japanese, it was at last the end of the war.

This Burpham party was for VE+50 in May 1995. Fifty years separate these parties but the sentiment is still the same, enjoying a celebration with your friends and neighbours, although at the start of the 21st century, a street party with sandwiches, jelly and cake is perhaps a thing of the past.

Reg Messer, president of Guildford Royal British Legion, at the Castle Grounds war memorial in 1975, receiving the wreaths of poppies in memory of soldiers who lost their lives in two world wars and those that have died in more recent conflicts. Mayor John Boyce can be seen laying the first wreath on behalf of the people of Guildford.

On 11 November 2001, Sue Doughty attended her first Remembrance Day ceremony as the new Member of Parliment for Guildford.

# Guildford People

It is not only the buildings and surrounding countryside that makes Guildford such a great place to live. People also play an important part in making it a pleasant town.

Over the past 50 years, through my business and privately, I have had the pleasure to meet many interesting people. This last section of the book includes articles on just a few of these people who, in their own different ways, have contributed something to the place in which they live.

## Michael Lampard

Michael Lampard and his wife Jean at a reception in the Guildhall.

One man who has certainly helped with the changing face of Guildford is Michael Lampard, pictured here with his wife, Jean, at a reception in the Guildhall. He is the senior partner of Lampard & Partners, the building contractors which he established in 1966. Michael was born in 1939 at the family home in Stoughton, Guildford.

He attended local schools and left Northmead Secondary School at the age of 15 to start work at A.B. Johnson as a bricklaying apprentice. Following his five-year apprenticeship he spent a few months at Pollard Bros, to get an insight into the plumbing trade, before doing his National Service.

The Electric Theatre, just one of the many building contracts undertaken by Lampard & Partners.

After his army service he spent six months with the building firm F.G. Minter before becoming a self-employed bricklayer in 1962. He married Jean at Holy Trinity Church, Guildford, in 1961 and they have a son and daughter.

In the 1960s, Guildford Council sold plots of land at Merrow Woods for local couples to build their own houses. Michael and Jean built their first home there in 1964.

The firm's reputation for working on listed buildings was established following their prestigious work on the restoration of the Guildhall for Guildford Borough Council. Some of their projects are mentioned earlier in the book and include Guildford House, the Undercroft, Burchatt's Farm and the York Road car-park extension.

Other contracts have included new buildings at the High School in London Road, County School in Farnham Road, St Luke's Surgery, Park Barn Day Centre and the refurbishment of Guildford Institute in Ward Street. The most demanding project was the Riverside development on Martin's Garage site in Millbrook, also mentioned earlier in the book.

The most difficult contract undertaken was retaining the existing façade of the old Gammons building in Market Street and North Street, whilst removing the internal structure. The conversion of 1913 electricity works in Onslow Street to the Electric Theatre in 1996 won the 1998 Surrey Historic Building Trust Award for best restoration to an existing building.

For many years Lampard's were sponsors for the town cycle races held during the Guildford Festival. They have also supported the Surrey Cricket Week and recitals held at the Guildhall.

In 1995-6, following consultation with his partners Roy Driscoll, who has been site agent on many of the Guildford contracts, son Steven and Paul Tester, it was decided to change Lampard & Partners into a limited company. Michael semi-retired in September 2001 and with Jean, both members of Guildford and Bramley Golf Clubs, plans to have more time for playing golf, his main hobby. Steven, Paul Tester and Mark Davis now run the company with Michael in a consultative role.

# Baroness Sharp of Guildford

Baroness Sharp of Guildford in her robes on introduction to the House of Lords.

Margaret and Tom Sharp.

Baroness Sharp of Guildford, known to friends and acquaintances as Margaret, has lived in Guildford, near Stoke Park, since 1984. She was born in St Margaret's, Twickenham, but her family later moved to Hadlow, near Tonbridge, in Kent. She attended Tonbridge Grammar School for Girls and went on to Cambridge University where she studied economics. Margaret subsequently joined the Civil Service and, whilst there, met her future husband Tom. They married in 1962 and went to live in Sydenham where their two daughters were born, in 1965 and 1967.

Education has always been of great interest to Margaret, especially equal opportunities for all in primary, secondary and higher education. As the children got older she became more involved, fighting for better nursery schools, and, in the early 1970s, chairing the Inner London Group of the Campaign for State Education. Her aim was to get more resources into state schools.

Margaret became a senior fellow at the University of Sussex in Brighton in 1981, working at the Science Policy Research Unit. Shortly after moving to this job she was adopted as Parliamentary candidate for the Social Democratic Party (or SDP) to contest Guildford's seat in the 1983 General Election. After moving to Guildford with their daughters in 1984, Tom and Margaret found their home becoming the centre of activity for first the SDP and later, the Liberal Democrats in Guildford. It was only late in 2001, after the successful General Election that year, that the Liberal Democrats set up an office of their own in Woking Road.

Margaret fought Guildford in four General Elections for the SDP and the LibDems – in 1983, 1987, 1992 and, lastly, in 1997. In a constituency which had remained Conservative since 1906, she managed gradually to squeeze the Conservative majority. The majority had been 20,000 before 1983 but by 1997 it was cut to 4,800 and this paved the way for the LibDem victory in 2001 when Sue Doughty became the new MP for Guildford.

After the 1997 election Margaret decided not to seek election to the House of Commons a further time. She continued, however, her role on the party's policy-forming committee and, in part in recognition of this, she was asked by Paddy Ashdown to become one of the LibDem members in the House of Lords.

Baroness Sharp of Guildford made her maiden speech in 1998 on 'fuel poverty', about the problems for the elderly poor over heating their homes and understanding how to claim allowances.

She says: "As a 'working peer' there is much to learn – a bit like being at a new school with all the new rules, written and unwritten. The first thing you get is a coat peg just like an old-fashioned school cloakroom."

After two years she 'moved up' to acquire a desk and telephone in an office shared with nine other LibDem peers. Margaret now spends three or four days a week in the House of Lords where she takes the lead for her party on education.

During his career as a civil servant, Tom Sharp dealt with topics as diverse as shipbuilding, bananas, trade policy and the privatisation of British Telecom. He also spent nearly four years as commercial councillor at the British Embassy in Washington, following which he was awarded the CBE. Tom left the Civil Service in 1987 to work for Lloyd's of London, and, in 1989 was elected as a LibDem county councillor for the Guildford South division. In 2002 he was still a county councillor. Having retired from work in 1991, he also served on Guildford Borough Council from 1991 until 1999. He is a governor of George Abbot and Sandfield Schools. He has also been a governor of Guildford College. Tom offers support to Guildford Symphony Orchestra and to Community Partners, the local self-help group, now Godalming-based, for those with learning disabilities.

In intervals from busy daily lives, Tom and Margaret Sharp enjoy walking holidays in Britain and abroad, go to concerts, do gardening, and seek to retain a sense of humour.

# Bill Broberg

This photograph shows the hairdressing salon of Percy (Bill) Broberg in Swan Lane in 1938. The entrance to the Seven Stars saloon bar is on the right. Bill Broberg was born in Gothenburg, Sweden, in 1907. He came to England with his parents when he was six weeks old and the family moved to Guildford in 1929. The same year his father bought the shop pictured above in Swan Lane, between the Doll's Hospital and the Seven Stars pub. Bill married Margery in 1937 and they had one son.

In 1938 he became owner of the shop and ran a gents' hairdressing business there until 1941 when he was called up for service in the army and the shop had to be sold. Bill was posted overseas and because of his connection with the hairdressing trade was ordered to cut his colleagues' hair. Bill protested that he had only been the proprietor not the barber. The army insisted that as he had seen men having their hair cut, that was good enough, he was now the camp barber!

He was demobbed in 1946 and his first job was with Coomb's Garage at St Catherine's. After Coomb's he worked for various engineering firms around Guildford and retired at 65 whilst working for Aerospace at Weybridge. It was during this period that Margery died. Bill rejoined Coomb's at Stag Hill, later Stag Hill Motors, and stayed with them until he finished working at the age of 85!

Before and after the war Bill played for Guildford Wednesday FC, so called because the team consisted of shop keepers whose shops closed on Wednesday afternoons.

Always interested in choral music, after he was demobbed he sang with local choirs including the Guildford Musical Society, Claude Powell Choir, Guildford Festival Choir and the Dennis Male Choir. He joined North Street Congregational Church Choir in 1946 and stayed with them when they moved to the new United Reform Church in Portsmouth Road. He sang with that choir up until the age of 92.

This was a scene from *Lilac Time* performed by the Claude Powell Choir with Guildford School of Music at St Nicholas Hall, *c.*1948. Bill Broberg is seated second from the left.

Bill Broberg with his second wife, Betty, whom he married on World Cup Final day in 1966. He attended two weddings that day. After singing in the choir at the United Reform Church he rushed to Wimbledon for his own marriage to Betty.

# Nikolai Demidenko

Nikolai Demidenko is a world-renowned concert pianist who moved from Russia to the UK in 1990. Although Nikolai has lived in Guildford only since 1993, he loves the pleasant character of the town and is happy to call it his home. He was proud to be granted British citizenship in December 1995.

Nikolai is a visiting professor at the University of Surrey and the Yehudi Menuhin School and at regular intervals gives recitals in the Performing Arts Centre at the university. He has strong views regarding the loss of the green belt surrounding Guildford and is especially keen to help preserve the character and quality of the town for future generations.

He was born in Aniskino, Russia, and started playing the piano at the age of two. He studied at the Moscow Conservatoire with Dmitri Bashkirov and became a medallist in the Concurs International de Montreal in 1976 and in the Tchaikovsky International Competition in 1978. He made his British debut in 1985 with the Moscow Radio Symphony Orchestra.

His concerto engagements have been numerous and he has performed with many famous orchestras. It is impossible to mention them all but they include recent performances with the Halle, London Philharmonic, London Symphony Orchestra, St Petersburg Philharmonic and Symphony, Israel Philharmonic and Singapore Symphony.

Recital performances have included appearances in Amsterdam, Belfast, New Zealand, the Paris Chopin Festival, at the Ford Centre in Toronto and the Valldemossa Chopin Festival in Majorca. He gives frequent recitals in London, at the Wigmore Hall, Barbican Centre and Royal Festival Hall. In 1996 Nikolai made his first Australian tour and in February 2001 made his New York debut at the Frick Collection.

Nikolai Demidenko and wife, Julia.

For Hyperion Records, Nikolai has released albums on the works of many great composers including Liszt, Rachmaninov and Prokofiev. For SanCtuS Recordings he has made albums of Schumann and Scarlatti sonatas.

His wife Julia is an accomplished violinist, and plays in the Northwest Orchestra in Golders Green, the London Schubert Players and the International Quartet. Julia also gives violin lessons at the Jacques Samuel Piano Showroom, Edgware Road, London, for 6–11-year-olds. Proceeds from a recent concert given by Nikolai, at St Paul's School, London, were donated to help subsidise violin and piano lessons at Hampden Gurney Primary School, helping to introduce instrumental lessons to a school which previously had none.

# Bill and Doreen Bellerby

Bill and Doreen Bellerby, pictured on the Guildhall balcony in May 1991, the year Doreen was Mayor of Guildford.

Bill and Doreen were born in Wales and came to Guildford in the early 1940s. He volunteered for military service in 1940 and was drafted into the Queen's Royal Regiment stationed in Guildford. A sporting accident, in which he broke his leg, prevented him from serving overseas and he was posted to the ATS training centre at Queen's Camp, Stoughton, as an instructor and orderly sergeant. This was followed by a short term in Ashford before he returned to Guildford where he was demobbed in 1946. Doreen, in the meantime, had joined Bill here and took a war job as a Post Office engineer. They liked Guildford so much that they decided to stay, even though they had placed a deposit on a house in Wales. Before the war Bill had studied to be a teacher and took up his first appointment at Northmead School in Grange Road. Having no family and with time to spare, Doreen started voluntary work. Her first experience was helping to set up an old people's club in Stoughton in 1948.

In 1960, after teaching at three other schools, Bill became head teacher at Knollmead School, Tolworth. Having never learnt to drive he became a familiar figure on the A3, cycling each day to school. He retired from teaching in 1979.

Following Doreen's involvement with the Nursery School Association, which brought her into contact with the Borough Council, she decided to stand as Labour candidate for Westborough and was elected in 1954. Bill started in Local Government in 1953 and was elected to Guildford Borough Council as a member for Stoke Ward, a post which lasted for 32 years.

Doreen's committee work included the Borough Housing Committee (1954-95) and, after her election to Surrey County Council in 1958, the Education Committee, on which she served for 20 years. This gave her the opportunity to join Bill on the Arts and Recreation Committee, overcoming the rule which prohibited husbands and wives from sitting on the same committee. Doreen has always been particularly interested in issues involving equality for women.

Bill became Mayor of Guildford and served for two terms – 1972-3 and 1973-4. During one term of office he injured his knee and needed surgery. Because of his duties as mayor, he asked if his admittance to hospital could be delayed until after Boxing Day as he would be busy over the Christmas period. On visiting the wards on Christmas Day he passed a cubicle with a notice saying, 'Reserved for the Mayor'.

He stood as the Labour candidate for Guildford in two General Elections against his old friend and adversary, Richard (later Lord) Nugent. In 1981 he was elected to Surrey County Council, for the second time, for Guildford North.

A magistrate for 20 years, Doreen became mayor in 1991-2. The same year Bill and Doreen were made MBEs and received their honours from the Queen together, as a couple. In 1991 they both received honorary degrees from the University of Surrey.

In 1995 they also received the greatest accolade the town could bestow upon the pair, the Freedom of the Borough. In the last 100 years there have been only 16 recipients of this honour. Between them Bill and Doreen have 84 years' service on the Borough Council.

People all over Guildford have much to be grateful for to Bill and Doreen Bellerby. They have worked tirelessly and unselfishly, not only as council members but also behind the scenes, showing kindness and compassion towards people in many different ways. When they both decided to retire from the council, their interest in Guildford life did not diminish. The couple are still fully committed to events concerning the borough, attending council meetings every six weeks but now, sadly, unable to participate. Even today they are both still making a big contribution to life in the town. Not surprisingly they have been dubbed 'Mr and Mrs Guildford'.

Bill and Doreen Bellerby, seen here wearing their Freedom of the Borough robes at the Guildhall in November 2001.

# Bibliography

**Alexander, Matthew** *The Guildford Guildhall. A Guide* (Guildford Borough Council, 1998).

**Collyer, Graham and David Rose** *Images of Guildford* (Breedon Books, 1998).

**Davis, Paul M.** *The South West Surrey Hospitals* (South West Surrey Health Authority, 1993).

**Guildford Amateur Theatre Association** *GATA Directory* (February 2001).

**Guildford Borough Council** *Guildford House (booklet).*

**Hamshere, N. and J. Sutton** *Happy Family. The Story of the Yellow Bus Service* (1978).

**Kelly's Directories Ltd London** *Kelly's Directory of Guildford, Godalming and Neighbourhood* (1965-6).

**Ockley, W.H.** *Guildford in the Great War* (Billings & Son, Guildford, 1934).

**Penycate, J.W.** *A Guide to The Hospital of The Blessed Trinity, Guildford* (1976).

**RNLI** *Sutton Place. The Art Treasures of Mr Paul Getty.*

**Rose, David** *Memory Lane Guildford & District* (Breedon Books, 2000).

**Rose, David** *Guildford Our Town* (Breedon Books, 2001).

**Sturley, Mark** *The Breweries and Public Houses of Guildford* (Charles W. Traylen, Guildford, 1990).

**Sutton, J. and N. Hamshere** *Safeguard of Guildford 1924-1984. Diamond Jubilee: A Pictorial Review* (1984).

**Sturley, D.M.** *The Royal Grammar School, Guildford* (1991).

*Abbot's Hospital, Guildford* (St Thomas's Trust, Guildford, 1999).

*Guildford Cathedral* (leaflet).

*The Bull's Head, Guildford* (Whitbread & Co Ltd, 1956).

*Royal Surrey County Hospital* (booklet, 1956).

*The Silver Jubilee in Guildford* (programme, St Catherine's Press, 1977).

Back copies of the *Surrey Advertiser*.